DECIDE YOUR FUTURE

Write, Direct & Star in Your Life

I0104383

CIE ALLMAN SCOTT

Foreword by

Michael Bernard Beckwith

DECIDE YOUR FUTURE: Write, Direct and Star in Your Life

For information address Dr. Cie Scott, 11811 N. Tatum Blvd., Suite 3031, Phoenix, AZ 85028.

Dr. Cie Scott's books may be purchased for educational, business, or sales promotional use.

For information please write: Dr. Cie Scott, Special Markets Department, The Wellness Docs Press, 11811 N. Tatum Blvd., Suite 3031, Phoenix, AZ 85028. DECIDE YOUR FUTURE; Write, Direct and Star in Your Life

FIRST EDITION

Allman-Scott, Cie.
Decide Your Future: Write, Direct and Star in Your Life

/ Cie Allman-Scott.

ISBN 978-0-9774811-5-6

To all who have taken the time to assist me and

support my endeavors to facilitate happiness and

success worldwide.

Acknowledgments

First, I would like to acknowledge my amazing husband, Aaron. He is the most influential person in my life. His Midwestern work ethic continues to fuel my own every day. My mother and father, Barb and Ken are most responsible for my start in life. Parenting is very under-rated in the world today: thank God for their sincere and loving effort. My husband's parents, Sherry and Norm are also major pillars of support; I feel deeply fortunate. I could not forget the friends I choose to support, and these ladies support me. I may forget one if I try to list all of my friends in Phoenix who inspire me, as well as friends in Los Angeles and around the world who I have known for meaningful periods of time; they have made my life incredibly fun and rewarding. My time is precious, so I am careful to choose well, and my friends are amazing. I thank God for this and so much more.

Special Thanks

I have been blessed with many inspiring and caring friends but I want to mention Jyl Steinback and Mary Contreras. These two ladies demonstrate hard work every day and never make excuses. I thank Heather Bushong back in Chicago for being the best, longest and most consistent friend I have ever known; she has unconditional love mastered. I will never forget the time Heather stood in line to meet Robin Leach at his book signing to ask him to cast me in a new show; Heather really understands how to support her friends like no one else. I will thank a thousand people in Hollywood for advice and lessons; Hollywood has its own school of hard knocks. I thank the great performers and comedians I worked with for our experiences.

I thank my teachers, of which there were many, especially Dr. Docker, ---I voluntarily studied 12 years past high school to become this unique person. I want to thank my High School German teacher, Herr Rheinhard Taylor, for demonstrating how students are engaged by a great performance, passion and humor. My father and Herr Taylor made it look like so much fun that I became an international keynote speaker. I thank my ministers, especially Rev. Dr. Michael Beckwith with deepest gratitude to Agape Spiritual Center in Los Angeles. The first time I saw Rev. Michael was the day my mind opened to see an infinite Universe that I did not fully understand, and I have been appreciating it for the past 27 years. Michael Bernard Beckwith is the most powerful speaker I have ever known and I love him dearly. He continues to inspire me all of the time. I want to thank Ernest Holmes for writing <u>The Science of Mind</u> and working to share his teachings with all religions, worldwide.

I wish to thank all the people of the world who take responsibility for themselves and their actions; they give me more free time and money to see this beautiful world and to invest in inspiring projects, and I appreciate what I learn from the rest of the world as well. Thanks to those who seek answers, seek the truth and find my bread crumbs. I am most grateful to be blessed and a blessing.

FOREWORD

It goes without question that everyone wants to be happy. What we do, what we say, and the choices and decisions we make are the pathways to which we think will lift the happiness quotient in our life. However, often we are flying blind. The questions we live with are anemic and keep us drifting through life experiences without much change. Our decision-making faculty may be dull and we end up living a life merely reacting to circumstances rather than choosing a path that will enhance us. But what if I told you that there is a way to making better decisions that can actually shift your perspective and bring more happiness into your life? What if I told you that you do not have to be a victim to the circumstances of your life and can unlearn habits that bind you while learning habits that free you? What if I told you that you are here to participate in your own unfolding and that you will not be perpetually happy until you consciously take this on?

Fortunately, you have made the decision to pick up this book by Cie Scott. Decide Your Future is a wonderful handbook to being deliberate in living the wonderful life that is seeking to emerge through you. It truly is a fast track to a happier life. Choose to read it, practice the principles, and then read it again. This decision will change your life for the better.

Richest Blessings,
Michael B Beckwith
Founder, Agape International Spiritual Center
Author, *Life Visioning* & *Spiritual Liberation*

Table of Contents

Introduction

Decisions, decisions. All of us are presented with numerous choices every day. Your life is the sum of your decisions. Small decisions are just as important as the big ones since many of them impact key aspects of our lives. Happiness is dependent upon making personal and appropriate decisions. Your relationships, health, and finances are at risk every day.

Would you like to be free to step into an empowered life and build success with every decision you make? Would you like to avoid the stress and struggle of making decisions? You can; this is actually not much to expect.

Simply stated, your life is a series of decisions. If you can make every decision powerfully and proceed from that place, you will find yourself at a more powerful place, and advance from there. If you want a better life, make better decisions.

We are often defined by our choices. We know and judge ourselves by our levels of success in each area or aspect of life, such as health, fitness, finances, work, family, relationships, and more. We all have strengths and weaknesses, but it is the weaknesses we accept in ourselves that hold us back and can be obstacles to making good choices. Self-doubt and believing in our frailties will undermine our choices, causing poor decisions. Unfortunately, the world is a judgmental place and how others perceive us can be as harmful as our own negative self-perceptions. Most human beings simply don't possess *bulletproof* self-esteem.

This book is a step toward being bulletproof; however, we don't want to emulate the sociopath, a bulletproof being that harms others. Unlike sociopaths, you can enjoy self-actualization and feel fulfilled with your life. Any form of self-hate or restlessness can dissipate. You will have victories, but not conquests that leave you hungry for more. Your creative energy will drive you into a joyful state.

There is a powerful, yet kind and gentle way to achieve all that you desire. Making customized, good choices will find you self-actualized, successful, and doubt-free. With a happy, wise, and healthy mindset there are many more benefits and dividends to enjoy.

Struggling with any issue is a sure sign that making a decision is imminent. For the 'tunnel-minded' that find it difficult to discern when it's time to stop 'forcing' an outcome, this will be a gigantic de-stressor and create openings. Surprisingly, surrender has a powerful place in life, and you will learn how to use it correctly in this book. What you chase will run from you; this is a very big revelation. In fact, it is a metaphysical rule. One of the aims of this book is to explain the role of appropriately surrendering. Often people surrender or quit too early, which is the leading cause of failure. Fear of failure is a gigantic obstacle in decision-making. We will clarify our doubts and fears and put them in their place as you apply my 7 steps.

For thirty years, I compiled data regarding dating and commitment. I did hour-long interviews with over 20,000 Americans on the east coast, west coast and the Midwest. Of all these people who desired to be in a committed, supportive, romantic relationship, most had been previously married or formerly had significant others. We revealed in every interview that each subject had the necessary information to avoid these failed relationships but previously made one (or more) traumatic, wrong decision. For many of us, hindsight is 20/20. So many resources and so much time is wasted when people make poor decisions. To avoid suffering—one of the keys for enjoying life— set your standards high. You see, life is full of important decisions.

This is not a book about studies of strategic decision-making or "game theory." Instead, you will be learning how to handle every decision with my fool-proof linear process. I will share some very interesting, sophisticated, scientific studies and findings from the psychological and business worlds, to explain why some decisions fail and some prevail.

Often, we do not decide when various circumstances occur. If we knew some decisions would lead to dreadful outcomes, we would have chosen differently. We will entertain the gamut of ways to make better decisions for the desired outcomes.

There are also no "shoulds" or "shouldn'ts" in the Universe. It is arrogant to assume that the outcome we desire is the desire of every energy force. Eliminating "should" from our vocabularies will save us grief and from eating our words later. Rather than struggling with this notion, just learn to stop using "should" for yourself, and as it pertains to others. Open your mind until the needed solution to the situation is found. When others are involved, find the 'sweet spot' where both sides can win. If both can't win, perhaps the decision is to walk away.

The thought of giving up the struggle regarding the challenges of life may seem impossible to most people. If you are one of these people, or know these people, examine the possibility of seeing things in suspended animation while sitting comfortably with the status quo before making a necessary decision. Agitation is a less powerful place in which to decide or implement something needed or new. You will want to face reality when you make a decision rather than doing it from a place of anger or disbelief. There is wisdom in stopping to take a deep breath. You want to make *good* decisions, right? Get centered rather than perpetuating the struggle. See what I mean?

Be completely honest, expose the truth to yourself, beginning where you are right now. First, relax and dismiss any need to fret. Acceptance has a simplicity that you will appreciate, but don't worry, because things are changing all of the time. Take a look at all that's good in your life, even if it's only one thing-life itself. This can be your launching pad. It certainly can be a place of gratitude, but also a belief that we have what we need to succeed. Faith solidifies this belief. Please accept that we all have a talent, an idea, or a way of being that others love; this helps anyone succeed. Additionally, right now each of us has an inventory of qualities that are good enough to get us through our difficulties. Where you are in your life is perfect, a difficult concept for some, but when you accept it, wisdom will follow. Just set your mind to see this perfection, accept it for this moment, and go forth calmly rather than struggling.

Quiet your mind of the chaos of the moment and simply accept that you already have what you need to get through tough circumstances. There is always a light at the end of the tunnel if you look for it. Opportunities are often disguised, and without a simple pause, we miss them.

OPPORTUNITIES ARE OFTEN DISGUISED, AND
WITHOUT A SIMPLE PAUSE, WE MISS THEM.

There is nothing wrong with feeling good about life. What is wrong with seeing a silver lining in a storm cloud? Every challenge is an opportunity to be uncovered. In stillness, sitting peacefully and undisturbed, the goodness or positive aspects of the challenge will come to you. We hear, "It's all good!" and it truly is. We grow bigger shoulders when we face our challenges instead of ignoring them. If we can be honest about where we are now, we can assess and progress. We have the choice to learn at all levels. We can find opportunities anywhere. People who aren't trained to seize these events miss capitalizing on them. For example, overweight people can make money by losing weight. Scandals bring forth healing that make excellent reading and big book contracts. Coming through a difficult time is quite inspiring to others. It allows others to feel that they may have power to deal with their own troubles. Each one of us can succeed powerfully, and inspiring others is a divine calling that is appreciated or marketable. In all circumstances, *"What doesn't kill me makes me stronger."* Accept this truth and it will also work for you.

We can achieve more in life by accepting our circumstances and using them as opportunities for growth. Don't fight it. Resisting what is occurring uses energy that we could utilize to create a better circumstance. Peaceful contemplation is often more effective than defending oneself.

There is a cost associated with not accepting life's challenges. The results people receive from complaining instead of embracing a situation create no benefit. In fact, struggling may create an increasingly bigger hole to try to escape. *Experiences that give us pain are a catalyst for our growth and success.* From a quiet place with a few deep breaths, we can make a decision with more clarity.

Every force of the Universe together will decide when the pieces of each puzzle will fit. With a Philosophy Doctorate, I will assure you, as we receive our answers by our successes and seeming failures, we are led to paths that contribute toward the greatest good. Sometimes it takes centuries of wars to clear up an issue. This is a deep and heavy realization; however, the steps in this book will work for small matters as well as serious issues. You will find that the results achieved in this manner bring the greatest rewards for any concern.

I love drawing parallels from martial arts or other physical activities to everyday life. There is nothing new under the sun. What works now also worked thousands of years ago. What works in karate works for all other aspects of life. What works in the dojo (place for learning karate) works at the office and at home. If we can master one aspect of life, feeling great, prosperous, and advancing confidently, we can use it as proof that success is possible in all aspects of life. It's true for every one of us.

Struggling often begins and continues for those who believe there is a separation that exists between people, places, and also that which they desire. There is no separation between people, places or things; everything is connected in the world and working together. We know this from the study of physics--matter and energy and their interactions. My husband's high school Physics teacher repeatedly said, "What in the world *isn't* physics?" Hold that thought as you learn some basics of metaphysics in this book. Metaphysics are at work whether you believe in the principles or not; similarly, gravity is always at work, even if you don't understand it. Metaphysics is another blanket, such as physics, which covers all circumstances. Spirituality understands that we are all connected, and what goes around comes around. That can be true for people anywhere, of any religion, race, age, or sex.

People that are well-practiced with spiritual beliefs don't waste their energy being flustered and angry. They go where life takes them. They know their purpose, and carry it out without fighting the current. In other words, they choose not to struggle.

Metaphorically, we are all waves in the ocean, and we move together interconnected, in a most perfect way. A wave in the ocean doesn't say, "Sea, come and get me wet— I feel so alone." We are never separate from any form of life, and it's eminently workable to follow nature's course. As strange as it seems, we have to flow, even during a fight. For a moment, consider fighting or resisting 'going with the flow.' As one lifts weights in the gym to gain strength and musculature, the last hard and heavy rep may not be flowing, but it's been proven that motion perpetuates motion. So, *use it, or lose it.* We will all be building muscles to make the best choices as we proceed with this book.

Studying anything from water to sports illustrates 'going with the flow.' You have seen great football players run for a touchdown, and as the opposing team attacks, they spin, rebounding off of the attacker and continue to the end zone for the touchdown. This supersedes the struggle. Struggling would result in a tackle, tripping, or dropping the ball. Water flows by jagged rocks just as it flows freely through a clean pipe.

Martial artists need not be defensive with their lives. Before I began studying karate, I was attacked four times, either to aggressively relieve me of my belongings or to assault me sexually. Over twenty years ago, while out of town on business, I was attacked in Miami. I was cut up pretty badly and had my belongings stolen. Broken glass was everywhere. I'd be dishonest if I told you I wasn't angry, but I decided to learn to protect myself and there hasn't been an incident since.

It must be the look in the eyes of martial artists that prevents others from attacking them. I don't look scary; in fact, lots of people smile and laugh when they see me. Martial artists walk the Earth like 'untouchables'. We don't show our belts, our licenses, or trophies for sparring. It's the air of confidence that tells the world, "Don't pick me. I'm not a victim."

You can do anything from praying to fighting without stress or struggle. You will understand these principles through the following examples. We can make any decision elegantly, from self-defense to 'tough love,' which doesn't enable others' unwelcome behavior. *Choices can be made in a graceful manner all the time.*

I have studied hard and soft styles of karate. I love the soft styles because of the fluidity and 'economy of motion'. While you perform a block or strike, one can use economy of motion to perform another strike, flowing with the last movement *in the next split second* to maximize efficiency. Building techniques that flow, doing more defense and damage with less movement is advantageous. For example, you can block your front side with an elbow that you can jam into an attacker's chin a fraction of a second later. Dispense less energy, increase the speed of the technique, and don't telegraph your movement before it hits. FLOW with it.

In life, why would anyone choose to use unnatural and manipulative acts, expecting them to succeed, or trick someone? These strategies eventually fail in the end.

Life always leads us forward in our own, individualized, perfect way. If we can simply show up with good intentions for everyone including ourselves, using our energy, intelligence, and spirit to create something, our ordinary selves become extraordinary. We can move mountains. In fact, the more intelligent 'would-be opponent' will not be able to derail us from our purpose.

As we learn to make decisions about anything without struggle, we can actually relax. Again, let's use physics and the study of motion to understand quantum physics and metaphysics.

The Three Elements of Speed and the Five Level Method of karate will propel anyone into success and popularity. Similar to when a great comedian is relaxed on stage, his timing is perfect, and the jokes are well-written and explosive. The type of speed that's effective in striking and kicking works in a job interview, a cocktail party, or training in the gym. It's the relaxation, explosiveness and independent movement (or technique done correctly) that project a winning blow. Grandmaster Jerry Smith passed down the Five Level Method, which works perfectly for any sport, activity, or event. It's a checklist of "success components." The following components for peaking physical, mechanical, technical, academic and psychological performances will allow an individual the kind of excellence that Michael Jordan has had in basketball. We call it the sixth level, *the spiritual level.* Some businesspeople make deals this way, and the best athletes play this way. Showing up prepared in every way makes a winner. In tennis, they call it being 'in the zone.'

We can all experience excellence in our lives. Half of life is just showing up. An empowered mind and spirit can make anyone unstoppable. We, as humans, must be open to the infinite wisdom of the Universe and see it as the 'big picture.' We can produce a product, or try to entice a mate, but if the effort is a failure, we must accept it. Roll with the punches, and try a new path. Life sometimes seems like a maze. We can learn to give thanks for the lessons as well as the successes. Life is an adventure, and not just designed for our comfort and convenience. Just remember to tell yourself that life is an adventure every day. Call those turbulent times 'adventures', and accept the direction they take you. You may see the good in it later. If you call it good, it can't be anything but good.

Trust the flow of the Universe and the bigger picture will be revealed at the time it will serve most successfully. Some choices are just stepping stones, but we may not know it at that time.

Graceful decisions and healing choices will always be for the good of everyone. Often, we are so engulfed in a problem, we can't see the answer, which will serve all involved. Even in a fight for your life, you can access 'the eye of the storm;' thankfully the eye isn't dangerous or turbulent. You can focus and make a decision, and it will be the right one for you. The sixth step will elaborate on this process.

Unbearable circumstances will be a catalyst to making a decision. Uncomfortable situations may also cause a change in a prior decision you made. Changing paths can be empowering. My parents lived and worked in an era when it was normal to remain working at the same company for 30 years. Now, living in the information age, progress and information travels so fast that we need to reinvent ourselves every several years just to avoid becoming obsolete. The Internet has bridged the information gap. We can now obtain sources for anything instantly. All businesses have evolved. Those who can make a decision to advance or change will prosper. You will learn to understand the timing for such decisions and changes. It is actually more comfortable to change than to be left behind without a way to satisfy basic and advanced needs. Those who avoid change may lose the little they have. Those who can't make a decision will have a guaranteed life of suffering. Because suffering is a choice, **suffering is optional.** You may also learn to change the frame around an event and see it as an opportunity, a blessing, or simply a rite of passage; this alone can alleviate suffering.

Integrity and empowerment are available in the life of any individual who has developed a high level of self-esteem. Loving the self is much easier than struggling with doubting and hating the self. This is absolutely true and easy to prove, however most people subconsciously hate themselves, which is the definite cause of so much struggle in the world. Lack of contentment causes people to find all sorts of conflict and trouble. Doing something positive for the world and doing it well is more the exception than the rule. I believe that 98% of Americans typically struggle in some way with finances. Many of the 98% can't recognize an opportunity or don't have the faith in themselves to create a lucrative entity for their talents, or they are not self-starters that can prosper doing what they love. All people have something they can develop that is incredibly unique and valuable. Maybe we can also add value to our world by advancing and making decisions to pursue the talents we possess. That is one of the aims of this book.

Deciding to love others as well as our self is another extremely important aspiration of this book. Another goal of the book is that it will open the mind of the reader to embrace new ideas. It is a privilege to improve upon current belief systems that may not be delivering the desires within any reader. There is no "have to" in life other than dying. I could illustrate this point with many examples. Cleaning your house is a "get to" of course. Living in a dirty, disorganized house is detrimental, whereas maintaining or evolving into a clean, living space is a "get to." As a second example, we "get to" go to work. This way we can pay for food, shelter, and clothing. *Get it?*

When we are born, there is no inclination within us that says we can't do something, have something, or be something. Most believe this is not applicable as adults. These beliefs are developed through experience, and most of us see them as a negative. Experience is another name for mistakes, which when you break it down are mistakes. We misspell, misunderstand, and mislead, so when we mistake, do what the actors do when they flub a line—have a good laugh and take it again. There is no one to tell you not to try again, although in some circumstances you may need to create a new chance, starting from scratch. *So what?* When we become afraid to try, we have allowed our self-esteem to take a dive and feel greater comfort in the realm of lowness or mediocrity. This is not how to attract a great mate or big money. You will always attract what you are. If you have hang-ups, you will attract partners with hang-ups. *Now you have twice as many hang-ups.* Here's the good news- low self-esteem is a falsehood. It is only a thought, and if you can change your thoughts, you can change your life.

As always, focus on the good. There are a multitude of things you have accomplished. List them if necessary. Don't listen to people who say you are doomed to fail. Choose friends and business associates who are not pessimists. No one can stop you from where you want to be, even if appearances seem otherwise. *There is no one who can stop you from getting what you want as long as you move forward with faith and people recognize your value.* Your accomplishments in an infinite world take nothing from others, so don't worry; being affluent hurts no one. There is plenty to go around. If you have any doubts, there is enough wealth circulating currently that everyone on Earth could live in opulence. Additionally, we can create more wealth; it's infinite.

Make the shift now to high self-esteem. You and your talents are worthy. Adopting the information in this book as truth and practicing it will raise your self-esteem. Poor self-esteem always gets people into trouble. Making choices out of fear is a sure way to be on the perpetual short end. Start anew by acting cheerful, even if it's difficult. Happiness begets happiness, I promise you.

If you're not happy, fake it for now. You have talents, accomplishments, and relationships to be grateful for *now.* If life or circumstances seem bleak, make a list of your achievements and you will then prove worthiness to yourself *with gratitude.* Look at this list before bed, upon awakening, or whenever you need convincing. Know that talents you don't possess can be developed.

There is cost to low self-esteem. Things you want will not come your way. You will only be presented with activities and opportunities of a *less-than-you-can-handle nature*. If you don't know your incredible powers, no one else will acknowledge or respect them either. Self-destructive behavior often stems from a low self-image. Think for a moment *why* people punish themselves.

You attract what you are. Don't attract depression and complaints. Try on happiness. It feels great and it fits perfectly. It's impossible to be sad when your head is high and you're smiling radiantly.

Are you starting to see yourself making decisions gracefully, happily, and without a struggle? I affirm that anyone can do it. Of course, it gets easier as you enjoy the results of the first few decisions. He who hesitates is lost. I don't hesitate. I don't miss opportunities, and I know that you can learn to make confident decisions that will serve the unique talents and spiritual design within you. You are entitled to all the good that life offers, so let's move forward and start to reap those rewards in life.

How to use this book

Read the whole book before you make your next decision. You can certainly benefit by recognizing steps you have missed in the past. Making decisions will improve your self-esteem when self-doubt is bypassed; this will be a big "confidence builder."

Pay careful attention to the chapters on Critical Thinking and How Your Brain Systematically Undermines Your Decisions. Faulty logic and cognitive short-circuits occur in all people. I know you will remember times you fell prey and made poor decisions when it felt right, and now you will find out why it felt right *yet wasn't.*

Hold your question aside, or 'table the question' as you read every step and apply those instructions to your question. If you have the necessary time available, this will be optimal.

If you are making a decision that is a "yes" or "no," do it or don't do it, this is going to work perfectly for this 7-step decision-making wizard. If you are looking for a solution to a problem, you may need to run choices through the wizard until it feels perfect. Start with the choice that seems most likely to work for you. If you hit a brick wall, start over with the next best choice. Because there is such powerful information in each chapter, you will find new solutions you hadn't thought of as you read.

In the medical world, there is a saying, "The enemy of good is better." If you are trained in the medical field, forget this for your decisions; the best decision is the best for you. The only challenge may be to get to the final decision within the time allotted, and this is one of the important steps.

Read this book repeatedly, or skim it as a reminder. It will become second nature to act in alignment with these steps.

When you understand the 'whys' of this book, you can cruise through every decision with the 7 steps, already taking into consideration the supplementary chapters. These chapters are great reminders and effective warnings.

"The illiterate of the twenty-first century will not be those who cannot read and write, but those who cannot learn, unlearn, and relearn."

~ Alvin Toffler

Decide to notice voluntary decisions that seem involuntary.

We are making decisions every second, with or without recognizing every voluntary action we take and every word we speak. These are all choices in which to earn rewards or reap unwelcome consequences. Simple choices like eating a cookie or yelling at someone will cause results, even without much effort or consideration. *Little decisions and actions add up.* Every word has meaning to someone. Perhaps many of us can gain new appreciation for *every* choice we make, taking greater notice. You can take greater responsibility with greater ease from now on.

Make a choice of these three options.

Complaining is a common everyday occurrence. We either initiate this act or overhear it, and it is a sign that a decision is necessary. If the same complaint surfaces repeatedly, *three choices are available to any complainer, and now is the time for a decision.*

1. CHANGE IT- Look at alternatives to a painful or unwelcome circumstance. You can use all 7 steps to make a powerful choice that will improve your life.

2. QUIT IT- Walk away or say, "NO. Enough of this." Do not allow this irritation in any form. Finish it off, let it go, and don't look back.

3. ACCEPT IT- If you can stop complaining and prefer accepting the irritation rather than the other two choices, this can work for you. I would not recommend accepting the unacceptable; this act will cause self-hating and suffering.

You have perhaps heard it before, but if you cannot decide to make a change, you may be accepting the unacceptable. *Why do smart people do this?* People behave in ways that make no sense because they are getting a 'pay-off.' When the subconscious mind is over-ruling a wise choice or a strategic change of course, it is because there is something else that the ego is selfishly protecting and will not let go. Pay-offs include the validation of simply being right (or affirming that it is the way the subject says it is), so the confirmation of feelings or opinions that something is terrible, has power and control over the mind. When people prove to themselves that something is terrible, rather than change courses, the ego gets to be right, but the person continues to accept the unacceptable. Becoming aware of this very human yet concealed and covert, thought process is the beginning of changing painful events and relationships in your life. Yes, these situations are controllable, but the emotional response (anger, shock, disgust, and/or confusion) fuels the way into a story that too many people decide to take on a 365-day, Broadway run. They want everyone to hear how bad it is, and this validation has power; *the ego loves it.* Your ego quietly agrees with what you are saying out loud, and there is some ridiculous comfort and satisfaction in that; it's extremely common. We will discuss more about the subconscious mind and how to take control of forces you cannot recognize within yourself; sadly, most people don't know they are engaged in self-defeating behavior.

Framing Your Question Appropriately Before Making the Decision

FINDING CONTEXT

Context allows the parts of a spoken or written communication that surrounds a word or passage to explain or illuminate its meaning. Context can also refer to the interrelated conditions in which something exists or occurs. In a different setting or environment, the context could have a completely different meaning. In order to fully understand and assess a statement, idea, or event, the context allows a better understanding of the terms. Sometimes, without background, we will not understand the factors or reference points that will properly frame the question. Improper framing offers an inappropriate question that will yield an inappropriate decision.

When we listen or read for context, the parts of something that immediately precede or follow a word or passage can clarify its meaning. Listening is a very underrated skill. Good listeners are certainly better decision-makers; this associates well with critical thinking skills. Master these skills. A misunderstood, poor communicator can become a champion communicator when they learn and practice better thinking, better listening, and better explaining. Describing the context well is an important key.

There are no problems; there are only challenges. Adopt this belief and see your blood pressure improve as you will solve those issues with greater ease.

The way we frame a 'problem' will influence the decision we make, and quite often, not understanding where to frame the question can result in disaster. When we articulate this issue, we are often using our own assumptions about the world to move forward by making a decision. It is easy to ask the wrong question when we are relying on the realm of what I call, "what we know that we know". Instead, including information containing the realms of "what we don't know" would very often change the question, the decision, and the results. What is the *real* issue to contemplate? For example, a surgeon would know options for appropriate surgical procedures better than a general practitioner or the patient, therefore the experience and education of the surgeon can greatly influence the outcome and help to frame the question to be decided. Obviously, such ultimately consequential questions related to health are best not decided by the patient without appropriate lab tests, scans, and multiple medical opinions, just to be certain to include all viable treatment options. This is true in all aspects of our lives; we cannot always frame the question well without knowledge outside our own understanding of an issue. Do you know how to do a Whipple? A Whipple is a long and complicated surgery also known as a pancreaticoduodenectomy, named for the surgeon who first performed it, Dr. Allen Whipple. The Whipple procedure is most commonly performed in the case of pancreatic cancer. After performing the Whipple, the surgeon reconnects the remaining organs to allow the patient to digest food normally after surgery. If you are not working in the field of medicine or cancer surgery, I can guess you have not heard of a Whipple. This is most likely in a realm of "what you don't know that you don't know". For me, a Whipple is in the realm of "what I know that I don't know". I'm married to a surgeon, and he informed me each time he was doing a Whipple; therefore, I know that it is a surgical procedure that is very long and complicated, but

I cannot do one. My husband knows what he knows and has done many; for him, a Whipple is in the realm of "what he knows he knows". These realms are three ways to relate to context.

Using a similar train of thought, a person may not need to know if they are compelled to get married to their significant other as much as they need to know if they are truly a candidate for marriage at all. You must ask the right question. Naturally, framing is very individual, just as decisions are personal; they are an individual quest for desired results. Poor results can be devastating. Your focus is key to framing the question, making a decision, and achieving desired results.

You may have a life-altering question that will affect the rest of your life noticeably? People change, circumstances change and your context will change, therefore your options will change throughout your life.

Decisions are influenced by Prospect Theory. This thesis was defined by PhDs, Amos Tversky and Daniel Kahneman. Prospect Theory demonstrates that a person will adjust their risk-taking behavior based on how a decision is framed; the mind assesses a loss as more significant than the equivalent gain. Also, a sure gain, known as the Certainty Effect is desired over a probable gain. A probable loss is favored to a definite loss; this is not hard to comprehend, but what is important to remember is that human beings tend to fear loss more than they desire gain, making fear a greater motivator than hope. One of the perils of framing effects is that people are often offered choices within the context of only one of the two frames, limiting context. It's stunning to think, with a little more information, a 'no' decision could become a 'yes.'

Individuals tend to frame decisions differently because of their perception. In this world, people are not all having the same experience. What people see in the world is actually their perception of it. Perception differs greatly from person to person.

Removing all of the biases and preconceived notions that have been developed through individual experience will be a great improvement; the ability to see and relate clearly improves the decision-making process and results.

Decide to be responsible consistently.

Life will change in a positive way when we notice that the little decisions we make add up to ugly habits. Patterns, nasty rituals and addictions keep psychologists in business. It is not your responsibility to support your local therapist unless you feel you are out of control. If you can understand this book, you *can* control yourself, and making decisions is what this is all about.

Why listen to me?

When I was a very young child, I dreamed of becoming a psychologist, a TV star and an international model. I did all of these things on a world-class level and I have accomplished more. Just like you, I have been told that my plans would not succeed. Sometimes with tears in my eyes, I moved to bigger cities and I beat down the negative voices in my head. You can do the same with your dreams. Like me, you can evolve to express deeper meanings and inspire others. You can take calculated risks *and a few more life-altering chances.* This is my plan for you. Allow me to share with you some of my efforts and experiences in hopes that you don't have to reinvent the wheel. A faster track has been built for you.

Who do you want to be? Write your script accordingly.

With every decision you make, remember who you want to be. In your current estimation, perhaps you are not this person you imagine. Hold a vision of how you want things to look; you can create your life and change things. Just as your brain has plasticity, and you have an ever-changing mind, you are an ever-changing person, unique and open for possibility. Let go of any residual victim story and your perceived limitations, then you can make decisions as you read what I have to share. Open your mind. Open your heart, and allow this book to convince you, if you have not yet adopted this belief. You embody greatness. If you aren't sharing it, let's find ways and open doors to start now.

MAJOR CONSIDERATIONS FOR EVERY DECISION

Contemplate these points as you work through the 7 steps.

When you realize how flawed the human mind is, you can notice patterns in your decision making that have not served you.

Correcting these patterns and glitches will allow you to be more successful in all you do.

When you learn best practices that supersede logic, your train of thought will flow with wisdom you didn't know you had.

Better thinking naturally yields better decisions and a better life.

WHAT IS CRITICAL THINKING?

Critical thinking engages the often-neglected abilities of the mind to come to correct conclusions about what is true or real, and about how to arrive at solid conclusions and solve problems. Distinctions of this process include:

- *proactively and skillfully analyzing and evaluating information to reach an answer or conclusion*

- *clear, rational, disciplined thinking that is open-minded and has been methodically conceptualized with evidence*

- *factually based analysis that discounts emotions and feelings*

- *purposeful evaluation, interpreted in context to form judgments*

- *committed and skillful thinking, used to clarify and organize data and form beliefs*

- *skeptical problem-solving that recognizes errors and biases in one's own thinking.*

Thinking is inward-directed with the intent of maximizing the rationality of the thinker. One does not use critical thinking to solve problems, one uses critical thinking to improve one's process of thinking, thus confidently solving problems.

Critical thinking has been defined as such for only around 50 years, but it derived its roots from the Ancient Greek. The etymology comes from two Greek words: "Kritikos" means *discerning judgment* and "kriterion", which means *standards*. 'Discerning judgment based on standards' is a short but concise idea of what critical thinking represents.

Critical thinking is not 'hard thinking;' it is skillful, organized, analytical, disciplined thinking. It enables problem-solving abilities more than defines a process to make decisions; it is a process to understand data. If you are on a search for the truth, this type of thinking can allow you to live in the truth and effectively direct your life. The more 'level-headed' approach is attractive because we are less reactive and more able to maintain enthusiasm for life.

When we allow ourselves to react as a leaf reacts in the breeze, we are not very substantial people. When the wind pushes the leaf one way, it blows the leaf in that direction, but then another gust or flow of air pushes the leaf in another direction. People really live this way. How can one not be exhausted with such emotional turmoil? Difficulties for people who think less and react more are many; staying on task, staying productive and just finding joy in being alive are interrupted. Critical thinking will allow anyone some much needed emotional maturity.

I am not suggesting to turn off your emotions. I am suggesting that we become emotionally mature and less flimsy than a leaf in the wind that constantly changes direction without plans or self-directed intentions.

Better thinking and reasoning will provide a better foundation for confidence and for every aspect of life. Call it an instrumental tool for personal development. It also allows us to evade the egocentrism and sociocentrism that clouds our judgment and cheats our intellect.

Your life is assuredly better when your thinking improves. Disciplined thinking elevates the thinker's life.

Those who would wish to influence us with slanted information will tell you that it is more graceful to allow your feelings to assist you in making informed decisions. But, economists and analysts would choose to scrutinize the facts, rather than be manipulated with feelings. When you are being sold a product, service, idea or policy, you are often told that you must *feel* your decision, but, this can result in being deceived and you will suffer some unintended consequences or need to revisit the issue when it rears its ugly head again. This occurs whenever the situation isn't properly addressed using a thought process. Sometimes you may feel better knowing that you did something that helped someone---*but did you actually help?* This process of disseminating information is used often in the political world where band-aids are expected to fix problems rather than assessing the cause of the problem and rooting out the problem before it continues to spread. In your life, you will suffer the same, so when you engage in problem-solving, it is important to analyze the real problem that undermines the condition. Unfortunately, we live in a world of 'spin', story-telling, and biased information. There is not one subscriber of the news media that believes that every source of news is unbiased, but once we know that it's challenging to find the truth, we can apply critical thinking skills to decipher what is true and not allow ourselves to be persuaded by distorted facts and unequal comparisons.

I aim to employ critical thinking skills *BEFORE* I allow myself to become emotional. Emotional reactions are certainly human, but it's very difficult to solve problems and make decisions when overcome with emotions.

As you work with critical thinking skills, you can show one emotion; you can be happy to know that you are the one in control of your mind. You can be joyful as you do not give away your power to those who would tell you stories that make you want to band-aid issues instead of search for facts and real solutions.

Early critical thinking is said to be recorded by Plato; they are, however, the teachings of Socrates. He presented that one cannot depend on government and those in authority to give sound knowledge and insight. This was true 2,500 years ago and is still true to this day. He showed that powerful people in high positions are frequently irrational and confused, despite their public, polished appearance. Asking relevant and in-depth questions can explore the base of knowledge before we accept this information as having merit to instill belief.

Socrates propagated the importance of seeking evidence, analyzing, and reasoning, and asking pertinent questions, known as "Socratic Questioning." Socrates insisted upon consistency in logic; the data must "add up" to be considered reliable information.

Aristotle later continued with this excellence in thinking. Examining our politicians and people in authority is difficult and time-consuming, but those who seek the truth will do it consistently and habitually. Most people in any country or culture do not take the time to do this. Naturally, we cannot have the kind of affluence and quality of life for all and that people demand when voters are not informed with enough actual knowledge to make sound decisions. Solving issues will require an army of critically-thinking voters. We must always remember that old saying, *"Believe none of what you hear and half of what you see."* Always question authority as the Greek philosophers did.

In your daily life, do you choose the 'short cut?' Do you partially engage in RARE thinking?

Research
Analyzing
Reasoning
Evaluating

Champion effort or even partial effort will improve your results for any aspect of your life. Try one example. Think about your body; what do you choose to eat and what can you gain from different types of physical activity, or sleep? *That is certainly another book, but learn what you can today and achieve some results sooner; it is certainly possible.*

If you do not, look at your personal results regarding your health and rethink your strategy. Apply this kind of effort to a few situations and see what kind of results are created. Relying heavily on information from friends or sources paid to disseminate data and advice is lazy and counter intuitive. Others are often sharing some 'hearsay' they just overheard, or in a more devious way, sharing what is personally advantageous to their own interests. Long ago, when I worked with my first personal computer, I was warned, "Garbage in-garbage out," and it applies so well here.

What is not Critical Thinking?

Three extremely relevant examples are given here. You will come into contact with all three almost every day from morning till night.

Do you use **logic**? Merriam-Webster defines logic as a science that deals with the principles and criteria of validity of inference and demonstration: the science of the formal principles of reasoning. *Make note of the fact that "critical thinking" is not defined by Merriam Webster at the time of this edition. I am hoping that critical thinking grows and 'lazy thinking' and assumptions do not prevail.*

Logic is a word from the Ancient Greek; it originally means "what is spoken" or "word," but it has graduated into meaning, *a subject of general laws of truth*, or, *to reason*. Logic would lead to a conclusion. It is ordinary to hear words like *hence* or *therefore* in typical discourse when logic is applied.

The scope of logic is not universally defined. We say things like, "There is no logical explanation for this." Well, it's great to think through the data, but all thinking is not equal or equally effective in the application. Logic has flaws at times and can be trumped by critical thinking.

Deductive reasoning is a form of logic. When multiple premises are combined, it is assumed that this correlation creates a valuable conclusion. It may not create fact but it certainly shows a relationship or related occurrence. It is known as 'top-down logic.'

Inductive reasoning is the process of taking bonafide observations and producing broad generalizations from that data. Inductive reasoning is called 'bottom-up logic,' but it is not considered by scientists to be a form of logic. Conclusions stemming from inductive reasoning can certainly be false.

Abductive reasoning allows the observations to conclude the best possible explanation. I would ask, *who decides what best is?* Best is quite subjective; two scientists may form different conclusions. When uncertainty exists, statistical inference can sum up a mathematically relevant conclusion.

There are holes in all these arguments. Perhaps it is best to study only the observation data and 'logical inferences'. These are the components and steps of logical reasoning, but instead of continuing down the path of logic, apply these premises to critical thinking.

Interim agreement occurs when a thought of some bias is widely accepted to a point at which groups of people believe it is absolutely true and have no hesitancy in sharing it. Without much thought, they perpetuate this concept or narrative. When people have agreed on a biased or unresearched thought, they have not used critical thinking skills to come to this conclusion; the end game could be embarrassing when the truth is known. This is why I do not subscribe to sharing thoughts that others have shared. Do sufficient research and think for yourself.

See the film Idiocracy. This comedy illustrates what can happen when people take cognitive short-cuts and an entire society devolves. Mike Judge, a prime-time, Emmy-winning writer, director, and producer created this film. Judge is also known for

Silicon Valley, King of the Hill, and *Beavis and Butt-Head.* And, I am not ashamed to say I support his craft with my Emmy votes. Laughter is medicinal, and we need it.

Storytelling is designed to supersede the need for logic or critical thinking by conjuring up emotions that can block important facts. I consider the other side when I hear a story; this helps me to find the conflicting issues with the point of the story. Storytelling is designed to make you feel so deeply that you will not consider critical thinking principles. I suggest that you engage critical thinking skills to understand an issue before allowing your emotions to overwhelm you. We spend far too much time reacting emotionally to events that are not presented to us truthfully, and data that is often deceptive by design.

To align your train of thought in making individualized, perfect decisions for yourself, critical thinking alone may not bring you to an ideal decision for yourself; it may bring you to a conclusion that is true and create a decision that will be more comprehensive. Importantly, using critical thinking skills will aid you in avoiding some horrible outcomes. When you choose appropriately, employing wisdom, there is no reason you cannot live at a very high, joyful vibration. (perhaps quality of life or lifestyle as many do not resonate with vibration and frequency belief systems/terminology)

Losing control of emotions can be very dangerous. Children usually use their emotions to make decisions; *this is why they need parents. (Human brains are not fully developed for optimal decision-making until about age 25.)* Being fully aware allows us to maturely temper our emotions. Juries have awarded people who have committed criminal acts huge sums of money because of the misfortune they may have both caused and suffered; this can be very unfair to the other side. Trying on the devil's advocate hat is not an act of pessimism. We must examine both sides always. Critical thinking allows us to be fair. Consider the act of revenge.

Being angry or feeling that we must correct an issue that didn't pan out well can create a terrible mess. You will become more aware and grounded and make decisions that truly serve you as you continue.

"Living well is the best revenge."

~ George Herbert

HOW YOUR BRAIN SYSTEMATICALLY UNDERMINES YOUR DECISIONS

I have been speaking internationally about the brain for about 16 years, and it is a continual audience mystifier, *and darn good 'info-tainment'*. It is surprising how highly-intelligent and educated audiences know so little about the typical performance of the brain. It certainly handles an amazing amount of data and animates your entire being with both automatic and intentional, subconscious functions. Most are unaware that a healthy human brain has what I would call 'blind spots,' and these glitches lead to constant oversimplifications, causing us to do things we would not want to repeat. Naturally, without knowing this, poor decisions result. It is normal for an educated and intelligent person to make poor decisions only because their healthy brain is operating as designed. When we become aware of these glitches and blind spots, we can overcome them and achieve greater results, as we might expect from ourselves. Learning about these default systems can certainly change your life by changing your decision-making process.

Physiological Brain Development

Science has recently shown that a human brain is not fully developed until around age 25. This is important because it is the pre-frontal cortex that matures the slowest, and it functions as the CEO, chief planner, and decision maker of the brain. It is impossible to believe that teenagers know it all when their executive functioning is still immature and somewhat undeveloped. It might be wise to rethink the mandatory ages for drinking, voting and other privileges that come with maturity. If you are a high school or college student reading this, please know that at your age I also used logic inappropriately, made some poor decisions, and my judgment was less than adequate.

In recent history we have the added effect of digital screen time. A $300 million study of 10,000 young people, known as "ABCD" is now concluding. Adolescents with seven hours or more of screen time per day, show thinning and aging of the brain. Two hours a day can impair language skills and lower thinking and developmental test scores. In addition, such learned computer skills that were thought to be educationally beneficial did not translate to the outside world. Consider the use of social media and the isolation some people experience; this can be a source of depression, causing us to live in a toxic state, both emotionally and physiologically, regarding brain chemistry. If you wish to know more, the Adolescent Brain Cognitive Development (ABCD) Study is the largest long-term study of brain development and child health in the United States. It has been rumored that Silicon Valley executives strictly limit their own children to the use of any computers, including smart phones.

How the Lobes of Your Brain Interact

We are typically able to successfully demonstrate use of many parts of the brain at the same time. For nearly a century, people spread the belief that we only use 5-10% of our brain. This is absolutely untrue. When this became public knowledge, and was shared with interim agreement, it was a distorted impression of the true ability and vast circuitry of the brain simply being underutilized, but this concept is invalid. It is much like saying that some people sit on their brains; while this seems valid, it isn't scientific and isn't true.

It is not unusual to drive a car, navigate to a destination and listen to the radio simultaneously. People are able to do this because some lobes or parts of the brain work together better than others. I ask my audiences to perform certain easy tasks, but in practice they find a surprising struggle; it's a bit alarming to experience, as it seems very easy when I explain the exercise. The Stroop Effect explains the noticeably longer reaction time of certain tasks and is often used to illustrate the nature of automatic processing versus conscious visual control. Named after John Ridley Stroop, the Stroop Effect was first published in 1935 following a series of undeniable findings from his experiments. Audiences find it enlightening. However, for this book, I want to share something more applicable for decisions. I want to share the issues that we cannot demonstrate and have been tricking us all through life. We have no idea how the brain and the psyche can work against us and instead, perform against, our best interest to get intended results. These are the blind spots we need most to understand in order to make better decisions. A wise person knows their strengths and weaknesses. Shedding some light on inconspicuous weaknesses can have great value.

Cognitive Biases and Detrimental Human Tendencies

To err is human, and these clear and defined cognitive biases are found ingrained in human behavior. Studies show that these biases can occur in almost any field or specialty in all types of people. Both experts and novices can be affected by these tendencies, and psychologists have witnessed their existence in field studies as well as staged experiments. Intelligence and IQ are not factors in who may fall prey. Flawed decision-making very often can be attributed to one or more of these biases and learning to counter these tendencies will strengthen your process and ability to make decisions.

Overconfidence Bias

Psychologists have shown that human beings are systematically overconfident in their own judgments. It's not always an unfortunate tendency that human beings are optimistic; it gets us through tough times and allows us to move forward but being overconfident and not taking necessary precautions or planning properly can result in setbacks. Judgment is impaired with overconfidence. Ironically, this can be coupled with poor decisions due to low self-esteem. The False Consensus Bias or Effect is another similar tendency in which subjects expect that other people think the same way that they do. To clarify further, subjects overestimate the extent to which their beliefs, values, opinions, preferences, and habits are typical for everyone and expected of others. In decision-making that includes other parties, we can see that plans involving others may not play out as assumed; this leads to a "false consensus." Lots of last minute, haphazard decisions are made with overconfidence and this causes accidents and even death. In traffic, overconfident automobile drivers believe they can beat a light or out-maneuver another driver with disastrous results.

Availability Bias

This can be attributed to laziness when thinking, but it seems logical and normal. Placing too much emphasis on information that is readily available at the time of making the decision will create skewed determinants that often result in a poor outcomes. Another attributed behavior is neglecting other applicable, appropriate information that can be found with additional effort. The human brain often accepts this lack of information with comfort and ease, without a second thought.

Framing Effect

This cognitive bias causes people to react to a particular choice in different ways, depending on how related circumstances are 'framed' or presented; it strongly correlates with Prospect Theory, illustrating how people will choose to avoid risk more than aim to make an equivalent gain. The framing effect can offer subject decision-makers a choice involving circumstances that appear to gain pleasure or avoid pain. Prospect Theory explains that losses are considered more significant than equivalent gains; this concludes that generally people want to avoid pain more than they desire to gain pleasure. This relates closely to the Distinction Bias where options offered together have different outcomes than those presented separately. When we are offered a way to take the easy way out, we often will accept this as a wise and logical play; so often better results are lost when situations are framed to be a time saver or advantageous.

Recency Effect

It is also common to weigh a decision more heavily on recent trends than a longer span of time that is more representative of what can occur. This bias can also occur due to laziness and can be rectified with more research. For example, we may associate good weather with the most recent trend; we may take better information for granted rather than reach for more reliable information.

Cost Sunk Effect

This is the tendency to make a deeper commitment to a course of action that has already received an investment of time, money, or other resources. Without appropriate, logical reasoning, people choose to "double down" or "throw good money after bad" in order to favor their prior decision, plan, or investment, hoping to finish with appropriate success. But, normally, these actions result in a larger loss. This bias is often seen in a casino, when losses feel unacceptable and doubling down may create the intended win, but the odds don't often yield the desired result. Cognitive dissonance might help to explain why "fixing" the original intent that is appearing to fail may relieve some mental distress.

Egocentrism

These idiosyncratic cognitive shortcomings neglect to recognize that others have differing perceptions. This effect occurs by attributing more credit to ourselves than an outside party would observe and attribute. This bias differs from the overconfidence bias due to the perspective and perhaps the point of view. For example, children at times believe that they caused something to happen by wanting it to happen. Egocentrism is often coupled with Magical Thinking.

Hindsight Bias

After the fact or the event unfolds, this bias is the tendency to judge events as easily foreseen when they clearly were not predictable before they occurred. Although actual harm cannot be done after-the-fact, it is irritating to hear that something was obvious to happen when that was not the case. As time passes, we believe "we knew it all along." This type of behavior robs the one assuming he/she rightly knew this information of a valuable learning opportunity; the lesson to see what was not researched could be used in the future for greater success. For example, "I knew she would be the one to get the promotion."

Confirmation Bias

Also known as confirmatory bias, it is the tendency to favor and interpret one's prior theories and preexisting beliefs, remembering selectively that wishful thinking and disambiguation are related. When two people with differing beliefs and attitudes attend a lecture, they may hear different things from the speaker that confirm their own opinions.

Self-serving Bias

In order to preserve the ego, perception is distorted to maintain a favorable opinion of oneself. Overlooking failures and overemphasizing achievements influence decisions and may include claiming responsibility for anything gone well. This bias reaches across all cultures and types of people. For example, an average employee that gets a raise or promotion will say that they deserved or were most aligned to receive this accomplishment.

Race consciousness and Prejudice

This judgment constitutes a positive or negative evaluation of another person based on that person's perceived group membership. Actual experience pays a smaller role than preconceived beliefs about the sex, age, gender, religion, ethnicity, disability, perceived beauty, or other class that influences errors in judgment. Since group membership does not indicate 'content of character,' flawed reasoning results. The old adage, 'you can't judge a book by its cover', applies. Without thinking about it, many people will feel most comfortable with their own race and join such groups accordingly.

> *"Few people are capable of expressing with equanimity opinions that differ from the prejudices of their social environment. Most people are even incapable of forming such opinions."*
>
> ~ Albert Einstein

Fundamental Attribution Error

Sometimes also known as the Correspondence Bias, people tend to under-emphasize external or situational factors while over-emphasizing personality-based explanations for behaviors seen in others. The 'Blame Game' and who should be faulted is a major result of this bias. We don't always know if someone is behaving a certain way due to their personality or due to their environment.

Illusory Correlation

This is the tendency to jump to conclusions by correlating two variables that are actually not related. At times, this has been propagated by not much more than superstitious or arbitrary circumstances that seem to appear related since they may have occurred in the past, but no actual relationship can be proven. A child may believe that all teachers are trustworthy and kind because her previous teachers have been.

Anchoring Bias

This occurs when a single reference point is allowed to distort our estimates; by adjusting the decision from this reference point, we allow ourselves to be influenced by a reference point that is completely arbitrary. This is another example of laziness taking us to an appropriate conclusion; the conclusion could be better served by finding several applicable reference points.

A negotiator or salesperson can use the anchor to their advantage; by using a high price, such as an automobile dealer sticker price (Manufacturer's suggested retail price) to begin negotiation; the buyer is at a notable disadvantage. If the buyer was anchored to the lowest price paid for the same automobile, the buyer would have a better bargaining advantage.

Satisfice

Think of this as a crossroads between satisfaction and sacrifice. This is the tendency to search for solutions long enough to find something acceptable, rather than finding the optimal solution with more effort. This behavior is extremely common and adopted so often due to time savings; the decision maker gets something acceptable and saves time, so it seems sensible, and like the biases listed, it appears to work. Economists know consumers will often adopt this behavior. We compromise what we want for what we are willing to settle for.

Systematic Bias

Poor estimating and systematic errors in measures or judgments are used to support or arrive at preferred outcomes. This is typically an institutional bias, and is also called as such. If numbers are a little off when you start a computation, the outcome of the study and resulting decision can be flawed due to inaccurate data.

Reasoning by Analogy

This occurs when we try to determine what decision to make based simply on correlations of similar situations that happened in the past. Drawing conclusions when being presented with similar ideas can nudge this type of behavior. "Since you loved that musical on Broadway, I'm sure you will love this musical as well."

Temporal Discount

The human mind is wired to take a smaller reward sooner than a greater reward for executing patience after calculation of each. Those who can accept delayed gratification have a discipline that will allow success that the average person will never experience. I previously mentioned Prospect Theory, where subjects prefer to act to avoid loss over a chance for a relatively similar gain. This very relevant tendency will be discussed in other sections of this book because the actual losses we can calculate are so numerous, including this theory of perceived losses.

Emotional Bias

Interfering with rational thought, this bias causes distortion of facts and decision-making due to emotional factors. It can cause a person to be reluctant to accept hard facts that are unpleasant to reflect upon. When a pleasant feeling is triggered, a person can neglect important evidenced facts. This is a function of being self-centered and is usually histrionic, reacting over-the-top; it is immature analysis regarding decision-making. In personal finance, investors often deal emotionally with stocks and make mistakes due to being overly optimistic or pessimistic. Frequently, investors are also lead by a bias of loss-aversion, which is considered to be emotional.

Hot and Cold Cognition

Hot Cognition affects reasoning and emotion; it is influenced by our emotional state. Hot cognition is triggered by the limbic system to make more of the 'reward" neurotransmitter, dopamine; this chemical messenger is often blamed for addiction and offers a rewarding feeling when triggered. The 'hot' sympathetic nervous system causes emotion to change the appearance of a subject or situation favorably. A mood ring is somewhat of a metaphor. Physiological and cognitive arousal are determinants for Hot Cognition. For example, important facts may be denied due to physical attraction to a fact presenter as much as the environment itself (very comfortable or uncomfortable) can affect the perception of the subject matter. Presenters offering food and drinks can create a warmer climate for enticing sales or influencing "buying decisions". This is why we can find cookies at an open house or popcorn at a car dealership. It's a welcoming gesture to entice buying.

Cold Cognition dictates that emotional involvement is not a factor. Logic and critical analysis are in play rather than influences of emotion or environment. Temptation remains in check and the parasympathetic nervous system rules. We can make better decisions, delay gratification for larger rewards and see a situation as if it's happening to someone else; this is another wise way to assess a situation.

If being in control matters to you, remember executive functioning in the frontal lobes of the brain would differ greatly when directed by 'hot' or 'cold.' "Cool as a cucumber" is the power position.

The importance of recognizing cognitive biases

You may notice that biases often occur due to laziness or arrogance, or enthusiasm created by a 'hot streak;' these influences are hard to avoid due to human nature. Just as nature abhors a vacuum, the human mind loves a shortcut and seems ready to act upon it. By and large, since making decisions is typically a non-linear process, it increases the chances of taking shortcuts, feeling inappropriately complete. The intention of this book is to create a more linear process whereby the reader can avoid these common human mistakes and make decisions confidently, knowing that all important data, as well as human inclinations, personal principles, and preferences were observed. With all these distinctions aligned, it is conceivable to be fully committed to your decision, with confidence instead of anxiety.

Is Cognitive Bias Modification (CBM) needed?

Certainly, it is important for teens to discuss important decisions with a wiser and more mature mentor. Being aware of biases and recognizing times when we have fallen prey to biases and prejudices is very important. Awareness is a necessity. If a person cannot access reality, certainly talk therapy and applied cognitive processing therapies can be used. Some people simply cannot find the truth. Some don't want the truth and these behaviors will be discussed in this book. Making great decisions will result in superior positioning, aligning the perfect situation for you. Your decisions advance you and if you are allowing covert operating systems to control you, your happiness, prosperity, and health are at risk.

Cognitive distortion and cognitive traps are numerous, and they solidify the need for a simple process or 'wizard'—-yes, *this book,* to calm these tendencies and allow for better decision-making using a simple process. There are many more tendencies to pull us away from the important factors for making decisions, so be aware of these compounding issues exerting their magnetic pull to distract and dissuade.

There are too many biases to mention in this text, but consider implicit stereotypes, jumping to conclusions, presumption of guilt, and magical thinking. When people have preconceived, subconscious expectations, these biases run amok and punch holes in rationality. There will be more to come relating to the ego and its inherent issues.

Indoctrination is another enemy of decision-making.

This process instills and instructs a person with ideas, attitudes, strategies, or methodologies without any critical analysis. This is dangerous to the subject of indoctrination because we are social beings that are shaped by cultural context, and the interjected beliefs may not serve the person being 'trained.' While parents and teachers are believed to be the major influences to indoctrinate, this detrimental process continues through the course of life, and our lazy, flawed brains allow it at all ages. Of course, the most susceptible are the youngest and oldest, but those who can learn to think and discern are hardest to indoctrinate. Beyond the vital function of forming stable communities, obeying laws and respecting others, people must think critically to overcome the ideas that are pushed by people who are self-serving or manipulative.

Suggestibility is a big, red flag that most never see. Studies show that subjects who are placed in groups with people planted to influence (known as *research confederates*); have their minds and attitudes changed approximately 30% of the time, even when they don't believe the newly-introduced information in the first place. This large fraction will surprisingly succumb to the influencers due to the need to belong to the group and avoid the discomfort of disagreeing. These startling studies show the dire need for self-esteem within every individual; humanity will be lambs to the slaughter if we cannot learn to independently think and discern facts from manipulated data.

Making effective decisions will mean avoiding peer pressure and overriding the need to conform. The influence of group-think is a truly limiting force. We must learn to think for ourselves. Don't mindlessly repeat what you hear. Letting others decide for you sometimes feels empowering, but it is more an act of fear. Think for yourself.

All of us have experienced some type of fear with making decisions. My dear friend and adopted sister, author Debbie Gaby shares in her book, "If you aren't sure of what your "steps" are to get to your happy place, it's okay not to know all of the answers; none of us do until we make the effort." Debbie would know. She is an entrepreneur who created a chain of mattress stores and returned 7 figure checks to all 10 of her investors. She now fearlessly operates her own foundation, Debbie Gaby Charities and raises funds for over fifty 501c3's in Phoenix, Arizona. She has also pushed past her limits, and you will be able to as well.

THE 7 STEPS THAT WORK FOR EVERY DECISION

Everyone can make decisions that are aligned with a personalized path to individual success ideals. Through this process, you will be assured and reassured of your decision, and you will not feel a need to change your mind.

STEP #1
Taking a Stand

Naturally, adopting a firm position about your issue will give you strength to persevere and ultimately build desired results that add up to multiple well-made decisions. In narrowing down your decision, you will need to build upon a foundation that directs your intentions and behavior. This foundation will be a demonstration of your values and principles. Your chain of reasoning must be sound and sturdy. Alignment with your personal expressed or yet unexpressed desires and intentions will make any choice easier to execute. Living in alignment with the person you truly want to be is the most effortless and most simple; this alignment also brings inner peace and allows us to live contented and happily.

At this stage, it's not necessary to shout it from the mountaintops or alert the media, standing for or against something, but it is important that we remain aligned to all that is near and dear to us; this matters in the grand scheme of your life. People that adhere to principles are the hardest to derail and the most truly powerful people.

PEOPLE THAT ADHERE TO PRINCIPLES ARE
THE HARDEST TO DERAIL AND THE MOST
TRULY POWERFUL PEOPLE.

Those who can decide to work on a cause without intentionally making enemies find that they recruit and accomplish goals faster than if they were utilizing energy defending or offending and conquering their 'enemy.' Paraphrasing, the late Rev. Dr. Martin Luther King said, "Wouldn't it be great if everyone stood for something, and against nothing?" King believed in something that was powerful for any truly loving and wise being; perhaps this is why his teachings live on and he is so greatly admired today. He adamantly adhered to spiritual principles, as Gandhi did. I cannot say he didn't experience opposition from unintended enemies, but at least today, we can say that his intentions were timeless and vast, and he took a powerful stand. If you are not sure how to take a stand, inquire into the lives of these men. They both demonstrate total decisiveness and an unwavering sense of commitment to their causes.

Think about the times that you have seen politicians change their stance to try to please *all* the people. At least half of the voters are turned off and poke fun at candidates that waffle. You may not be able to please everyone, but you also don't need to offend anyone. Honestly, most of your life's decisions will affect you or your relations. When you live powerfully, and your words inspire others, the sky is the limit. Many people may be affected by your decisions. All decisions, big and small, require a firm stand. For example, your kids won't take you seriously if you punish them by grounding them, and then lift the sentence prematurely. Your children will not benefit from discipline that is rescinded. Instead, your children will learn that your decisions are not firm and that you can be manipulated. Employees need that same solid decisiveness. Making flimsy decisions will ultimately result in lost respect in the workplace as well.

"Carefully watch your thoughts, for they become your words. Manage and watch your words, for they will become your actions. Consider and judge your actions, for they have become your habits. Acknowledge and watch your habits, for they shall become your values. Understand and embrace your values, for they become your destiny."

~ Mahatma Gandhi

The average child begins life possessing all the admirable qualities that they need to get through life happily. When we were younger, we were more imaginative and vulnerable. When we were children, we opened our arms and hearts to everyone. But, every time something negative occurred in our life, we formed a shield over ourselves for protection. Consequently, we often treat others based on negative past experiences. We need common sense more than we need shields of any kind. Unfortunately, defensiveness and cynicism get us nowhere, and hold us back from progress.

There are strong and weak people. Which are you? If you feel vulnerable or allow others to make your decisions, step-by-step we will build your personal power.

We have taken experiences in which we played the victim and told the stories as if we were decorated soldiers for surviving these incidents. We know we will never be canonized for our survival. We can just be thankful we lived to learn the lesson. Later, we find these stories we told just confirmed how silly and small our lives were then. Our time is better spent working on the relationships and opportunities that are available today and in the future. We waste our valuable time by rehashing the past. We could spend that otherwise wasted time by enrolling people into the vision we are creating for the future instead. Enlightening and enlisting people into your cause will strengthen your stand.

Hearing and buying into others' victim stories is just another draining, waste of time and energy. If we love our friends, we know they are more powerful than the person in their stories. How many times have we repeatedly told these stories to others? Sometimes it's hard to catch ourselves in the *woe is me* mode. Have you wondered how most doctors and nurses handle sick patients and don't contract these illnesses? It seems amazing that hospitals are staffed by professionals that don't become afflicted with the diseases they treat. The caring professionals solve problems *above* the level of the problem. They don't get sucked in. They approach problems clinically in order to help. Getting involved in others' problems on the same level will not help anyone.

> *"The significant problems we face cannot be solved at the same level of thinking we were at when we created them."*
>
> ~ Albert Einstein

Living suspended in time and controlled by fear is no better than retelling horror stories from our pasts. The saying, "A coward dies a thousand deaths" explains how anxiety can affect our lives. We may not think of ourselves as cowards, though we could be procrastinators. In any case, we suffer so many times just imagining possible disasters, we could have made a play for what we have been anxiously contemplating, re-hashing and fearing. The suffering of failure could not be more debilitating than all the internal struggle and misery of doing nothing. Sometimes advancement is just learning what does not work. Mistakes are just another term for experience, and experience is very desirable.

When we actually think through the scenario I just illustrated, we can create a custom mental exercise; this will allow us to push forward rather than handling the misery of the self-imposed restraint of doing nothing.

Let's try it.

1. Choose something you want to do but are putting off for a later or more appropriate time in the future.

2. Consider the poor results you can achieve and allow yourself to feel the failure. Visualize the pain or anguish you will feel if it doesn't go well, *or if you do nothing to change it.*

3. Consider yourself successful with your endeavor. Feel the joy you would experience if you had succeeded. How would your life be? What would you be doing right now? How could you improve lives of those you love?

4. Having contemplated these things, can you put your reservations and fear aside?

We can benefit by monitoring our behavior and noticing when we procrastinate. At that point, it's important to ask our self why and conquer these thoughts or fears. We actually suffer when we allow ourselves to come up short. We must not allow our thoughts of doubt to influence us to wait. Right now is the right time.

Judgment about what is 'bad' can make you feel sick, or worse, be the cause of bodily disease. Focus on your decision and what that will translate to be. Other's beliefs are no less valid, but does it matter? All beliefs are only interpretations; on the positive side, beliefs can be launching pads for valuable results.

Your impressions and calculated probabilities about what is likely to occur may be very skewed, and we will address that. Making progress for your cause takes a firm, confident stand. You have heard the saying about the turtle, a seemingly powerless creature....

"Behold the turtle. He makes progress only when he sticks his neck out."

~ James Bryant Conant

You have a decision to make. Are you taking a stand? Can you visualize yourself taking a stand for what you want to materialize? If you cannot, perhaps you will find the strength later, as you read further about the decision-making process. If you would feel empowered, joyful, or even satisfied with your desired outcome, keep your aspirations and contemplations alive.

'Taking a stand' and 'taking a stance' differ, but both are relevant. A stance is a posture or the way you stand or position yourself; it is also taking a side of an issue.

Commitment and the faith of your convictions may be challenged. When you stand at a podium or atop a soapbox, be warned that people may try to pull you down. Even friends and family may not appreciate your vision and choose to like the "old you" better than your stronger, newer self. Fortifying yourself with undeniable facts, integrity, and clear objectives will make it much more difficult to pull you down from your soapbox or your plan.

To be respected, be certain that your facts are solid, proven, and will serve to help others. Too often I see people take a stand with logic that does not add up or is in some way damaging the framework that is needed to uphold it. After you apply critical thinking skills and the steps in this book, I fully trust you will not justify a weak premise and you will stand firm for something of value.

> *"Genius is the ability to hold one' s vision steady until it becomes a reality."*
>
> ~ Benjamin Franklin

Every human life can benefit with a purpose statement, also known as a mission statement. Before you finish this book, this will be readdressed, and you will have what you need to write a firm declaration of who you are. This is also applicable for companies and other organizations. This statement is for your structure and alignment, and you will enjoy the benefits of taking a stand for something meaningful.

The Benefits of Taking a Stand

Like-minded individuals will identify with you and give aid. Others will be attracted, and they will be those you would like to have to participate with you. You will sleep well at night as you speak your truth.

The Implementation

Decide with your heart which side of the fence you choose, but always get the facts straight so you cannot be steamrolled with better research. Always speak with conviction when you are trying to promote something. Be honest and forthright. Honesty will allow you to avoid flimsy words such as *probably* and *maybe* to be sure you are understood and attract the right people to yourself; don't allow weak self-expression.

The Cost of Living without Conviction

Manipulating others by playing both sides will create an unwelcome and unexpected backlash eventually. Confusion will clutter your mind. If you are making an important decision, you can believe that it won't 'stick' without commitment.

Know what you know. Speak your truth and you can enroll assistance, and perhaps also allegiance.

Nike doesn't say, "Just try it." It's "JUST DO IT."

**STEP #2
Integrity Always
Matters**

Why is integrity important? The first rule of integrity is to be true to yourself. It is vitally important to keep your word to yourself and uphold your own values without wavering. Staying true to principles will be a recurring theme in this book. How can we begin to keep our word with others if we cannot keep our word to ourselves? Start with yourself. Notice if you make promises to yourself, and for whatever reason, you do not keep your promise as this shows a lack of integrity. Keep your promises, uphold your values, and when you consistently believe in yourself you can believe in your dreams. When you are able to walk with personal integrity, you can begin to walk with integrity with those around you. Your realm of possibility becomes greater and your results reflect success.

When we are aligned with righteous principles, honor, and a general completion of responsibilities, we feel connected to all other people. Upholding our word means never losing sleep due to your conscious or subconscious mind. There is no guilt. Why wouldn't we keep our word? Why would we not do our best work? Why would we be late? We want to be aligned, the way a wave moves in the ocean with other waves, rhythmically and easily.

Integrity is extremely attractive. Let me illustrate how it can influence others. Time after time, as we confirm to others that we keep our word, show up as promised, and act honorably, people will decide they like us, *or certainly the people you would like to participate in your life will show up for you as they understand the importance of this trait to you.* Others perceive the consistency you demonstrate as steady and calming, and this benefits everyone.

Integrity and self-esteem are strongly correlated. All patients that have come to me for any psychotherapy know how to use integrity to heal self-doubt or self-hate. Allow me to share with you how to achieve high self-esteem. It' s highly valuable yet an inexpensive lesson that is life-altering.

- Walk your talk.

- Keep your word.

- If you say it, mean it. Don't talk because you like to hear your own voice. You will find that the use of integrity, starting with these simple suggestions will prove to you that you are aligned with high ideals. You will begin to think highly of yourself. As you continue with these practices, you will enjoy who you are. You will not want to harm yourself. Some of us know that liking ourselves will cause behavior that is healthy. Many people cannot be alone; it is painful when you don't like yourself on the subconscious level. Thankfully, I have known addictions to be overcome with this form of self-love. Others around us will sense that we like ourselves, and they will appreciate us more. If we treat ourselves well, others will treat us well, too.

Your integrity and self-esteem are connected to self-love. This association will definitely influence your decision-making for the better. People that love themselves work hard to achieve a better life for themselves and others. It is also inspiring.

Tune into inspirational people, places, and things that are geared to improve your life. Take notice of ways you can better your existence. When you see beautiful photos of models or bodybuilders, this is not cause to be jealous. The editors of magazines and producers of TV don't use beautiful people to initiate jealousy. Experiencing hurt in this form has little to do with the object of envy and everything to do with feelings of inadequacy. If you feel this type of pain, you can choose to be inspired instead; this is another chance to reframe your point of reference. Use people who would target your jealousy as an example; appreciate them rather than curse them. Know that if it's possible for them, it's possible for you. Do you believe Oprah Winfrey believed she would not make it as a TV hostess because she was not as worthy as Dinah Shore or Sally Jesse Raphael? I think not. Did Oprah believe that because she was sexually abused as a child, she had no right to all the good the world offers? I think not. Shaquille O'Neill inscribes everything with "TWISM" which means "The World Is Mine." As a Lakers' season ticket holder, I had many years of celebration and elation due to Shaq's talent. Everyone has something of value to share. We can't say that looks, brains, or connections must be present to have success; it is your unique talent and consistency that achieves success. I can offer loads of examples of people who decided to believe in their abilities, or they believed that *not* achieving was so unacceptable that they would not quit until they achieved. When we want to create certain results, we can ask these successful people how they accomplished their achievements. I will tell you repeatedly, you don't have to reinvent the wheel.

By beginning with one step toward these ideals, we improve our lives. With each subsequent step, we achieve more love for ourselves, and it tends to exude toward others. You cannot receive more respect from others than you give to yourself.

Many people want to have their own TV show, yet no one ever asks me how I created that reality in my life. Things are usually not what they seem, so it's important to research and ask questions. When I wanted to improve my physique, I asked everyone at my gym about how they achieved their progress and built their shapely parts. Half of that information turned out to be very valuable to me. My enthusiasm and admiration for their success opened doors for me. It doesn't pay to be shy when you can inquire and learn. When you ask politely, and your hero feels your admiration, they will be very happy to share their path with you; it's a compliment. Proactive people will accomplish more than reactive people. If you're waiting for something to happen, stop waiting. If you have a good excuse, forget about it and move ahead on the path anyway. Your energy will be met by the Universe. What goes around comes around. Make it positive. These ideas and lessons feed off of each other. Practice them if you have not yet done so.

"Men occasionally stumble over the truth, but most of them pick themselves up and hurry off as if nothing happened."

~ Winston Churchill

Set yourself up for success and the payoff of higher self-esteem with every decision. Use the complementary chapters in this book to align these puzzle pieces and decide to do what you can complete on time and with valuable end results. Each demonstration of your excellence will bring forth more opportunity.

Please choose to follow excellence. Do not allow yourself to identify with most people.

The Benefits of Integrity

When a person is in integrity, the world feels perfect. There is no struggle. It feels good to keep promises and excel at one's purpose. This chain creates more mutual support. *Expanding the integrity of the Universe increases what is available in our circle of existence.* Choosing integrity instead of withholding our best effort is a certain way to make our own lives abundant.

The Implementation

To incorporate integrity into one's way of being is to release discomfort in one's life. Simply do well for everyone you agree to do work for or work with in partnership. Do your best at home with family or roommates. Do things the way you prefer them done for yourself, on time and as professionally as possible. Think of doing and creating *not as a sacrifice*, but a pleasure and as an expression of your existence, and the world will be enhanced. *Improving others' lives always comes back to the giver.*

Think about your decision and how it will affect your life and the good that can be built upon that decision. Will you perform in integrity, and how will that pave your way to greater things?

The Cost of Living without Integrity

Be certain that no impropriety reflects upon you or your work. Does your decision reflect that you are responsible and honest rather than double-dealing or underhanded? On the other hand, knowledge that you are involved may not be optimal for everyone associated. In other words, you can give a gift without signing your name to it. As long as you know that what you have done was either responsible or appropriate, this is all that matters.

Withholding from others will demonstrate in your life as a withholding from you. You may notice this and monitor it in your life. If you can't be reliable as a source of productivity, this decreases all you wish for that's within your reach or available to you. A feeling of discomfort occurs if you don't keep your word, excel at your purpose, or do your part for others. If you know this feeling, allow this discomfort to push you higher from now on.

At any time, anyone can choose to live in integrity and feel connected to everyone and everything they desire.

STEP #3
Timing is Your Window
of Opportunity

When must your decision be final? Is this the best possible time to share this decision with others or would everyone benefit if you adjusted this time or date? Make a commitment to serve yourself and others by finalizing your issue.

You have heard, "Timing is everything." I don't think it's *everything*, but the wrong timing will trash a great idea or proposal. Timing can also turn a great and powerful decision into a useless, expensive, or powerless one.

If you choose not to answer the phone or your emails when you are not busy, this is something you can change to keep your life fresh instead of stagnant. It's time to *align with your life---because you are obviously trying to separate from it.* If you don't like what you have started, decide to say no, but don't leave people and issues hanging. Timing must be addressed; you don't want to take your chaos and spread it like a disease, do you? Return phone calls. Answer your phone in the first place, whenever possible. Be decisive in a fair amount of time or have the decency to ask for a determined amount of time if you don't have enough information to decide what you are doing. You always have the freedom to pre-set others' expectations if you are busy and cannot answer quickly. This is a matter of organization, so align with your life instead of trying to escape. If you are guilty of this, then decide not to be a flake and bring some order to your life immediately. This behavior is not only disrespectful to one's self, but also to others. There is no upside to unnecessary time delays.

ORGANIZATION sets PRIORITIES, removes CHAOS, and provides FREEDOM.

Timing can create stress and these correlated concepts can help you with timing. Set priorities. Be organized. Reduce your stress.

"All things are ready, if our mind be so."
— William Shakespeare, Henry V

Our decisions are best made and implemented at the most beneficial time. We must learn to assess opportunity as well as allow change to flow at the most advantageous time. Life will not always consider your comfort and convenience, so set your priorities. Decisions made too early cause confusion, and if you're late to decide to act, you may miss the luxury liner. I say that you miss your big chance if you don't move forward at the right time, in other words, you may 'miss the boat', though, sometimes you will find a dinghy.

Let's consider an example to illustrate preferential timing. People often attract people if the timing is right. When I met my husband, we were both looking for the right person. When I saw my husband, I had the spooky feeling that he was 'the one.' I had no idea who he was and had no prior knowledge of him. I told a couple girlfriends about my discovery minutes after I saw him. Naturally, they thought I was crazy. He didn't even notice me. A month later, he walked into my office, talked to me for an hour, and then asked me on a date. I did not disclose my intuitive belief until the time was right, many months later. This behavior of good timing was absolutely necessary. He is not a needy person and he would have run if I had shared that little tidbit about the first time I saw him. Let's assume you have just met the right potential partner or spouse. Knowing it intuitively, having done a background check on him or her, with all risks calculated, and following every other rule, you would not want to propose marriage on the first date. That early proposal could blow a perfectly good beginning out of the water. The perfect start could most likely be destroyed. If you have that mutual attraction, due to great timing, you can see how valuable it is to continually work with appropriate timing. Mature people do not appreciate what seems to be immature or needy behavior. The potentially great spouse wants someone who is levelheaded, not a flash in the pan---here today, gone tomorrow.

Most timing errors are not the case of being too early. Procrastinating and stalling are the major causes of lost opportunity. A good decision will open up to opportunity. Poor timing constitutes inadequate decision-making. I remember after dating my husband for six months, I warned him that I would not wait forever for him to set a date for our marriage. I desired marriage over simply being his girlfriend. I was a good catch and I knew it. He knew it too, therefore, without manipulation, he acquired a ring and proposed. He preferred traditional marriage over dating perpetually as well. He didn't want to miss the chance to create a great proposal or a great marriage; however, at that time, the jeweler lost the ring. He proposed to me with a ring that was quite ugly just so he could 'submit his offer' and utilize magnificent timing. I thought the ring was horrible, but the guy was great, so I said yes. To my surprise, a month later, I received a fabulous ring. I think I can also be credited with a good decision. Most things in life are not perfect, but timing and doing something loving, wise, and positive will always win. Timing is something that we can often control, so we will create a better life when we don't procrastinate.

Worry, doubt, and fear cause procrastination. Laziness also facilitates this stalling behavior. People that are lazy don't deserve a luxury liner; they deserve a dinghy. As I was getting dressed and watching the news this morning, I saw a commercial in which the narrator said, "We all deserve a vacation." This is not true. Those who have worked at something worthwhile, saved the money, and have the time off deserve a vacation. Everybody deserves the right to the pursuit of happiness. Everyone does not deserve happiness. The U.S. Constitution and God do not guarantee happiness or a vacation. These things are earned. Being lazy or fearful will slow down the completion of work or responsibilities and minimize free time. We cannot allow excessive fear to hold us back. Most people will allow fear to ruin good opportunities.

You may say, *"WOW. You would take happiness away from someone who does not deserve it?"* The truth is, we all are worthy of it, but we create our lives with our decisions, and we must live in search of the truth. I don't say any of this in a religious way; I advise to find out what isn't working and change it. I stand for everyone to be happy and prosperous; this is the world I would clearly prefer to enjoy.

In many cases, it is laziness that inhibits our happiness. In too many cases it is the subconscious mind that is the procrastinator, stifling action and all the good the world offers.

Fear of loss is a powerful motivator and a major indicator in making decisions, or more likely *not* making decisions. I can assure you that procrastinating is a powerless reaction and commonly people lose their window of opportunity by avoiding the decision. Remember, the thought of gain is less powerful than the fear of loss for most humans.

Fear of loss is usually an illusion that seems valid. It is also common to lose something while trying to preserve that very thing, or a related person, item, or circumstance. So often we are focusing on the wrong thing (the fear of losing), and in doing so, we sabotage what we want. Fear of loss impairs timing very frequently if not regularly.

> *"It's not that I'm so smart, it's just that I stay with problems longer."*
>
> ~ Albert Einstein

People often quit early. This is another error of the timing distinction. People don't get instant results because they have not had the time to earn the desired result, but they will prematurely quit a proven program, simply because they aren't an overnight success. Most people are 'overnight successes' *years in the making.* When we see a new movie star who is seemingly, all of a sudden popping up in lots of films, believe me---it could have taken them ten, twenty, or more years to position into this success. I have interviewed hundreds of movie and TV stars and 9 out of 10 times, they started with puppet shows or school drama club and community theater. Most stars attend years of classes, invest large sums of money to build their skills, and reap the rewards later. If it was easy, everyone would do it. Most of them didn't mind being waiters and taking odd jobs to pay bills while they waited for the right opportunity and the right director to cast them in a hit. Their families made sacrifices for them to become these 'overnight successes,' occurring over years, not overnight. Much of what we can see is an illusion; get used to it. Hard work builds wealth, relationships, and good health. Working hard and working smart are good choices for now. Eventually, when you have racked up several great decisions and are reaping the benefits, you can work smart and not work hard.

Procrastination is the result of a lack of faith, consciously or subconsciously. This feeling can be a lack of faith in the plan, but more likely, it is a lack of belief in the self. The old *"Woe is me" and "I can't"* will predictably take a good plan and turn it into nothing. This is true for most people. Is this true for you? If other people are succeeding where you are failing, you aren't giving it your heart and your head. I have seen more people succeed with heart than smarts. It is that heart that I call the "Infinite Power."

You may not say the right words, but if people know you believe in what you are doing, that message will be conveyed, and it will overpower words or actions that appear weak. Remember, we don't really fool people. Presenting in an inspirational manner and at the right time will draw the elements needed and pay out over an imperfectly executed proposal. When you see your opportunity, get moving. Don't wait for what you think is your perfect time to do it.

Work on it while it is still an opportunity. Again, this is why 2% of Americans can do whatever they like and the other 98% may be wondering why they don't deserve better or have decided to accept a life of less prosperity, love, or health.

Let's examine what happens when we wait. Prices of many things increase, putting them further from reach. We live in the Information Age; therefore, things change rapidly. If we don't use today's information today, we lose our chance to capitalize or improve circumstances. When we have made a weak decision, we can't expect to reap the desired outcome.

Hesitating, delaying, and agreeing to seeming obstructions will not allow us to advance. Most obstructions are molehills appearing to be mountains. An acronym for fear is False Evidence Appearing Real. Does that resonate as truth to you? Fear is a powerful debilitator that anyone with a sound mind can overcome. Michael Jordan, the former NBA player said, "Fear is an illusion." This may be a good mantra to regurgitate every time you seem to be caught in fear. My former next-door neighbor and best-selling author, Susan Jeffers, Ph.D. wrote <u>Feel the Fear and Do It Anyway</u>. I highly recommend this timeless wisdom to fear sufferers. *Since the first printing of my book, Susan has shuffled off the mortal coil and I will miss her friendly and helpful nature; she was blessed and a blessing.*

First, we must differentiate between fear and danger; this is apparent when calculating risks. Some people decide to accept physical danger in order to earn more money. This is a matter of risk and reward. There are many things we can choose that put us in no physical danger, but we must be willing to accept possible rejection, which is an entirely different risk. Most people can't handle rejection because they have so little self-esteem that they cannot risk the little bit they have. The ego is delicate for so many folks, but the ego is not an effective tool to use while making decisions. If you are in this fragile category, and by statistics, it is likely that you are, decide now to build high self-esteem. All aspects of your life will bloom when you think yourself worthy, confident, and strong, and see yourself making a difference by improving something on this planet. Indeed, confidence plays a huge role in timing. Confident people have far less issues with timing. People who aren't confident will allow a wide array of reasons or excuses to impair their timing.

"Don't watch the clock; do what it does. Keep going."

~ Sam Levenson

Are you 'timing impaired?' Do a self-check now. Are you waiting due to any of these?

- a lack of financial backing

- a lack of contacts or people to enroll into a wonderful plan

- false evidence that appears real, fueled by a lack of confidence

These indications may ***not*** be important enough to delay you.

Around 2004, I met Ralph and Cathy Oats; they are very inspirational and definitely self-actualized. They founded Wellness International Network, and I have taken several of their nutraceutical products as well as been to their palatial home in Dallas. Becoming so successful was an undertaking in timing and overcoming fear. Ralph did not wait to have a degree in health or nutrition. Ralph was a truck driver and Kathy was a housewife and mother. They made a decision to sell water filters for a multi-level marketing company, but they did not allow their poverty to stand in the way. They went to a bank to borrow $5,000 to buy their inventory of water filters. They put up their home and car for collateral. Ralph was terrified, and to make matters worse for them mentally, the banker told them they were crazy to attempt this venture. In a few years, they became top producers for that company. They not only became millionaires themselves, they created hundreds of millionaires in the process of helping their personal finances. They pushed forward despite the negativity that people spewed onto them. This negativity was intended to help them and advise them not to waste their time and risk their scarce money supply. The moral of the story is *don't let a bunch of people influence you if they don't know how to be successful in the first place.* Now they live across the street from Ross Perot in a palace that strongly resembles Versailles outside and the White House inside. Sometimes, people who are starving or having severe problems are the best at prioritizing change. In these cases, they know they need change and need to survive. It can be a blessing to be desperate. Although change is difficult to create for most people, many of the richest people were born poor. They despised poverty more than change so they implemented something that would free them of poverty.

Waiting in poverty doesn't work well. A new life is a decision away. For countless people, poverty was a blessing, and they used it to fuel their decision to change.

So often, family will try to talk us out of something and try to influence our decisions when they really don't know how to achieve the desired outcome. This exercise is a waste of time. We don't need to assess opinions from people who don't know what they are talking about, even if these opinions are well-intended. This is the time to write-off such advice. If you want to know how to be happily married, ask some people that have been happily married for 50 years. If you want to be a millionaire, don't ask someone who is working at a job, paying a mortgage, and can't afford all the vacations, charitable contributions, and possessions that are on your list of goals. Make your decision and utilize optimal timing. The time is now to start in some way. Simply declare the path and where you are going.

For all the time we spent making excuses, we could have created the potential outcome we desired in the first place. We must learn to identify the time we waste contemplating failure. Instead, do your due diligence and get started or choose something better. Make a decision instead of mulling over reasons that something may fail if you choose to get involved or make a commitment.

Waiting has many frustrations. By doing instead of waiting, you may fail here and there on your path, but you will meet people and discover other open doors. Stagnancy is expensive, too. It can cost you your dreams.

You can sometimes be early, but you don't want to be late. People are often late paying their bills. Most people are behind in attending to their other personal business. Most people are disorganized or can't think well enough to make a decision because they don't choose to focus or cannot manage priorities. Speeding up the process by using these rules for making decisions will allow us to idealize timing instead of procrastinating.

When we delay a decision, this is not progress or building an intelligent conclusion, it's procrastination. Most people know right away what their decision is, but they allow doubt, fear, and worry to cloud the next stepping stone to their happiness.

You won't have to worry about being admired if you are not decisive. By not making a decision, you can be depleting the resources that you are trying to preserve. These items can be money, friends, or the respect of others. If you can't get to work, how many people will want to work with you? If you can't decide to get married (or formally commit) to your great potential spouse after sufficient timing, what message are you sending? It appears you are still searching for someone better. If you aren't sure, *who is it that you aren't sure of?* Is it the potential spouse, *or is it you?* Apply that question to any situation and take another step toward a better utilization of time. Time management is just another choice. Some people attend classes to learn to optimize their time properly because it is critical to our lives. When I don't see progress in my own projects, the stagnancy drives me crazy.

Take the measure from your own shoe. Do you willingly choose to do things with people who can't make up their mind? After you are frustrated, you will move on, right? If you are not progressing, you will throw them on the back burner, stop calling, and leave a non-decisive person to their own devices. I am a mover and a shaker, and all my close friends are movers and shakers. They might make an occasional mistake, but it makes for good dinner conversation and a good lesson. When people move forward or shake things up rather than making timing the excuse, they will succeed often enough. Sitting on the couch, rehashing strategies endlessly will not create valuable relationships, good health, or admirable finances.

We hear about politicians 'kicking the can down the road,' which is possibly a lack of decisiveness, or likely to be politically expedient; perhaps they know that to solve a problem, they will lose some support, and this is unacceptable. Political types find it easier to spin the story about making the decision than actually solving a problem. Problems can be solved but this will not please everyone. A wise person can see it happening, and a wise person notices if it is part of their own modus operandi. Problems only escalate when no action is taken. Dealing with such people would be madness, *so don't expect me to run for office.*

Why do we have trouble moving forward with a good thing in a timely manner? Everything we do is ruled by the subconscious mind. Consciously we may want something and may be willing to create a change to get it, but a monstrosity of old experiences, including little images or flashes of everything we have ever seen, heard, or experienced, will influence the behavior; this influence is rarely good. Our minds are always storing this detrimental information, as it happens in our lives. We each have our own file boxes of images and impressions to influence our behavior, which are remembered and regurgitated back through the mind constantly. Everyone who ever said, "You are not good enough," is in there. Any time you failed at something, it's in there. Every negative thing that your mind ever processed has been stored in your own personal chatterbox. It then comes back out telling you, "You can't work this," or "That's too big for you," and your behavior chooses to follow the negative thoughts over the positive thoughts. There are ways to overcome this. You can learn to think positive and shut down the chatterbox. My chatterbox also slowed my behavior and decisions, but you can be more powerful than your past. I will explain this process in coming pages. It is important now to notice when you allow yourself to be slowed into submission. In a changing world, we don't have time for our past to haunt us.

Timing contributes to LUCK---Living Under Correct Knowledge. *Again*, in a changing world, you don't want to be *he who hesitates.*

"Life is about timing."

~ Carl Lewis

The Benefits of Appropriate Timing

We profit or gain exponentially by aligning ourselves with exciting opportunities of all kinds. Being organized and ready is valuable for every aspect of your life.

The Implementation

Now is the time to let go of excuses that cause procrastination. Make the act of being late an integrity issue in your life. Good timing is just as important as keeping your word. Never leave people hanging.

The Cost of not Utilizing Appropriate Timing

You miss opportunities. You may create disrespect for yourself or anger people you love. It is guaranteed that your finances will not thrive if you are disorganized. If you are slow to take care of your health, you will lose your strength, flexibility, and physical condition.

Timing mixed with awareness has created incredible wealth, fantastic relationships, and glowing health. Make the decision to focus on your timing and reap these rewards and more.

"You don't have to swing hard to hit a home run. If you got the timing, it'll go."

~ Yogi Berra

STEP #4
Calculating Risk is a
Must

We can calculate risks for all aspects of life, not only in business. It's important to weigh the benefits and possible consequences of an action before the decision is final.

Put on your "no risk=no reward" hat. If you don't leave your home because you are avoiding pain, risk, or decision-making, get serious about this step so that you can increase the potential of your life exponentially.

Do you dream of a perfect relationship, with an exciting and supportive person that warms your heart, loves, and understands you? If you think this is too lofty a goal, I concede that there are no perfect people, but you can definitely find the perfect mate. You are the perfect mate for your perfect mate.

Maybe you have not calculated your risks that govern your health. Calculating these risks can cause you to make better decisions for the rest of your life, and benefit others in many ways as well.

By taking calculated risk, many have created unbelievable fortunes. Would you like to be financially rich? If you are not excited by the thought of being rich, remember, freedom for your loved ones is also a benefit of financial wealth. Get excited about this possibility that is now open to you.

In a biography of hotel magnate, John Q. Hammons, written by Susan Drake, I found a quote by an unknown author: **A Golden Rule for Success: "I want to take calculated risk, to dream and to build, to fail and to succeed, to turn my back on security in search of opportunity, and never be numbered with those weak and timid souls who have known neither victory nor defeat."** This is what it would take to be a hotel magnate, but the same rule for calculating risk can aid anyone in finding the success you desire, big or small.

Calculating **break-even points** in business is quite simple. If your break-even point is considerably low, you could hit the profit margin sooner. Get it? When the risks are low, *get ready and go.*

Now you know that numerous studies show that people are twice as upset about a loss as they are happy to enjoy a gain. This is a sad state of mind, yet so typical. These studies show that individuals tend to opt out of risk. The Ellsworth Paradox illustrates this; people predictably aim low and settle for mediocre results rather than aiming high to achieve more. A military analyst, Daniel Ellsworth did experiments in **expected utility;** he designed games of probability with colored balls in urns. His experiments showed a relationship to demonstrate how people react to volatility, uncertainty, complexity, and ambiguity; people generally avoid ambiguity and uncertain odds. If people were perfectly rational, they would realize that risks that are only half known are not known well enough to avoid. People sell themselves short on a predictable basis. We typically focus on the possible losses instead of striving for unguaranteed gains.

The Ellsworth paradox reliably predicts human behavior for the majority. A strong example illustrates that it's preferable to be miserable in a job 'for the security.' People sell out most of the time and could have better control over their lives and earn more if only they could be more comfortable with uncertainty. Faith is typically lacking.

What we are left with is a typical brain and a decision-making modality that is wired **to choose safety,** *even at the expense of happiness or wealth.* More advantageous decisions may not be a difficult reach, but the reach seems too painful.

The first test for calculating risks is simple. Just think of the worst things that can happen and list or make note of these. Is there anything on the list that you could not accept as a possible outcome? If nothing is unacceptable, it's a seemingly easy decision. Also list what can be done to mitigate these losses, then reconsider.

Here is a simple example of this rule in use. If I want to gamble in a casino, I decide how much money I can afford to lose. I limit that amount as my risk. I may be rewarded if I win, however I have decided how much I can risk and lose without being angry with myself or not paying bills. For example, let's call this amount $100. I would not be angry with myself if I lost $100, so that seems acceptable. I can also agree or decide to play with $100, and if I lose it, it will simply be my cost of entertainment. With this prospective or 'frame' I will not lose sleep if I lose $100. I can accept the worst thing that happens. Casinos rake in loads of cash because people are not disciplined to stop, but I calculated where I wish to stop, win or lose. We will revisit this scenario later.

My health is very important to me. I choose not to smoke because I cannot accept shortness of breath, smelling bad, and lung cancer as possible outcomes. There is no upside for me.

I enjoy drinking wine with dinner. If I drive to a restaurant, I choose to take into account that I could get a DUI or DWI for drinking, which I cannot accept. I don't want to spend 2 nights in jail or kill someone. I do not want to break the law, lose my license, and ruin my professional reputation. I do not want to spend time as well as money to go through the court system.

The outcome of the drunk driving punishment is absolutely unacceptable. I choose not to risk it. *I still take more risks than most people, but they are calculated risks applied to meaningful situations.*

All things in life should be so easy. Let's move forward to more complicated calculations.

I met a man and fell in love, and now he is my husband. I had to regard certain factors before deciding to marry him. If we get married in a community property state without a prenuptial agreement, I could be responsible for any bad investments he makes. I could have a broken heart if we get divorced. My life could become very complicated and I might have to move to a smaller place, or rent instead of own, or live with my parents or roommates. These are the risks. What could I gain? I could be happier and healthier in a marriage. My life would be more defined and easier to navigate. We could have a happy family and have greater finances combined by living together. We could honor each other with a binding commitment that could feel more comfortable than growing old alone. What are some of the deciding factors? Both of us have high integrity and are highly dependable. We have both been previously married and have ideas about what we do and do not want to create. Neither of us is addicted to anything. My husband and I are both above average at earning money. We both spend money the same way and do not accumulate debt on credit cards. My decision was therefore not very difficult. Due to the consistent behavior of my husband before we married and our agreement on all issues, risk was very low. Had he gone through bankruptcy a couple times, I would have had increased hesitation; factors such as this matter to me. My husband had one other way of assessing his risk. He hired a private investigator to look through my finances and my past to see if there were any red flags.

He and I decided to get married without the difficulty that most people face. Being in love or finding your soul mate is not reason enough to become married without considering the risks.

James Z. Joyce said, "A man of genius makes no mistakes. His errors are volitional and are the portals of discovery." I mention this to illustrate that there are no truly bad ideas. Even failures are useful when you learn a valuable lesson. In order to take risks at all, we must often break patterns.

In order to assess risk, we must always have reliable information. It's nearly impossible to make the best decision when working with data that is intended to manipulate, but often we cannot discern this easily. Take nutritional supplements. The U.S. government will allow pharmaceutical companies to make claims about their products but nutraceuticals cannot make claims. Notice the way that these products are sold to you; they tout certain results for certain people but cannot make across-the-board claims regarding their intended results. Instead of mimicking the pharmaceutical companies, nutraceutical products resort to testimonials and storytelling. Users of the product rave about how the product changed their life, "and it can change your life, too." This is the pitch, and storytelling has proven to be quite powerful and convincing. A testimonial story without any side-effects might be much more convincing than actual drugs with potent active ingredients. Pharmaceutical drugs are required by the U.S. government in all pharmaceutical advertising to list any side effects, and some of these are quite negative. Do your research and assess those risks.

Many people could be at the same place at the same time and recount things in a completely different way. For example, a beautiful woman, a shy woman, a guy who drinks to excess, and a womanizing man all attend the same party. The shy girl says the party was humiliating and terrible because she didn't talk to anyone. The heavily drinking guy says the party was great and he can't remember a thing. The beautiful woman says it was awful because so many guys were bothering her. The womanizer says it was terrible because there were only three girls and thirty guys in attendance, *and the three girls didn't go for his lines.* Possibly, if one of the girls would have taken a romantic interest in this man, he would say it was a great party. Odds are that most people had a nice time and were glad to have attended. Every day we listen to many more interpretations than facts. We can learn to separate proven fact from interpretation and lessen concerns heard through interpretations, consensus, or opinions. Don't allow a lot of negative talk to slow your progress. Get facts and take action proactively.

What is true in fact must have the capacity to be proven. It needs evidence more reliable than what is testified in a court of law. Testimony is actually very weak and cannot be considered solid proof. Can we believe others? Always consider that the message we hear is a personal interpretation. Is this information reliable enough to judge? Beliefs are often simple judgments.

What is the truth?

Science exists to construct proven and accurate knowledge about how the world works. The word "truth" is sometimes used to refer to spiritual truths or other topics that science cannot investigate. If you are a scientist, you may also use the other meanings.

There are many meanings for this word and it is used in different contexts, so I will clarify. "Truth" is:

1. (a body of knowledge) The truth is all of the facts about something, including any facts that surround it. It is the body of real, evidenced things, events and facts that are based in reality. For example, "Scientific data shows the truth about possible side effects."

2. (noun) an idea or judgment about that which is proven. "These are truths of investing in the stock market."

3. (adjective) faithful to a promise/fidelity, consistency or sincerity in action, character, or words—-"This product is tried and true." "He is true blue."

4. (a religious belief system, seen capitalized) with reference to God's word in religion or spirituality — "a witness to the Truth" has meaning reflecting upon God and God's vast word, not one account or one proven reference to an event that happened. It is common to believe that this is not a scientific truth because it cannot be investigated, but concepts are being formulated on this subject all the time to prove that spiritual laws work just as laws in physics work. Stay tuned on this subject. "New Thought" explains how spirituality and science come together and offer Universal teachings. Based on religion and metaphysics, it began in the 1800's in the United States and advances modes of healing the mind.

For this book's purposes, I will use truth as a fact that is proven. I like to use truth as something proven at a specific time (or consistent at all times), at a place (or everywhere/universally) but very well evidenced, *not a theory, even if well-correlated.* I like my truths to be quantified, evaluated, appraised and computed accurately. I expect that if something is the truth, however you add it up, the answer is the same, without exception. If you see Truth capitalized in this book, it will refer to a Universal Truth, a spiritual principle that is true for all religions and non-believers. I would capitalize anything referring to the goodness of God and the order of the Universe with respect to the Creator. (With this said, if you don't believe in a Creator, laws of the Universe work for absolutely everyone anyway.)

One thing is certain; most people are allowing flimsy facts to suffice, skewing their conclusions and covertly lowering their standards. When you calculate risks, please require verified, bulletproof facts. I don't accept truth and facts that can be shot full of holes.

Plato first documented his desire for the truth. He was deeply concerned with testing for the truth as an indisputable fact, proposition, or principle, confirmed as the issue needed. Truths demand the mathematical works to be defined in terms of time, space, and distance. Socrates, Aristotle, and Plato called it "veritas;" this is Latin for truthfulness. Veritas is the Goddess of Truth in Roman mythology. She was a daughter of Chronos, the God of Time, and the mother of Virtus. The meaning of Virtus was to possess character, valor, excellence, and courage, which were considered manly strengths at that time. *I chuckle; the world has evolved.*

Hearsay

Hearsay is not fact, but it is often treated as fact. It is usually someone's unverified story about collected data that may amount to no more than a rumor or gossip. We have all watched a courtroom scene in movies or television in which the witness is being questioned after taking an oath to tell the truth. (This alone is ironic; many people don't know what truth is, and what it is not.) Often this witness will swear he saw something, and we find out that he does not have his facts straight, even though he may fully believe what he is saying. Actually, witnesses are the absolute worst type of evidence for a court case; humans stray much farther from truth than physical evidence, yet we are to believe that these witnesses hold the keys to the decision or verdict, and some are so confident in their testimony that they'll say, "This is the truth!" Hearsay is not a strong and reliable source of information for many reasons. I give these reasons without intending to insult anyone's memory, credibility, or integrity. The human memory, blessing that it is, is faulty, and it often rewrites itself. Yes, it can and does, even when testimony or any sharing of information occurs. If you didn't know this, I am certain this is shocking news. Look up or search false memories, indoctrination, and the misinformation effect, and you will learn how surprisingly unreliable the words of seemingly reliable people can be.

Sadly, it is acceptable to most people to permit personal accounts and stories told by others to be assumed truthful fact. Stop allowing this. It is imperative that this is not data for your decisions.

Know more than the other guy, or at least do your due diligence.

Economics, insurance, and risk management use **adverse selection**, a term that describes a situation where market participation (of buyers and sellers) is affected by an information imbalance, called **asymmetric information**. When buyers and sellers have different information, traders with better private information about the quality of a product will selectively conduct trades that benefit them the most, taking advantage of the other side or other trader. A textbook example is George Akerlof's paper, The Market for Lemons: Quality Uncertainty and the Market Mechanism, written in 1970.

Of course, used car dealers know whether a car is sound and well-cared for or a 'lemon,' and they are able to over-charge for cars of poor quality that break down constantly. Naturally, doing a 'win-win' deal is optimal for too many reasons to list. Sadly, people continue to be cheated every day.

George Akerlof received the Nobel prize in economics for his findings, and almost 50 years later, every US state has its own version of the "lemon law" to protect consumers. The United States also ratified a federal lemon law, known as the Magnuson–Moss Warranty Act to protect citizens of all states. We still make bad decisions, not just in purchasing goods, but widely and commonly. There is really no excuse for this. Often, it is simply human laziness.

Naturally, the party without the information is rightly concerned about an unfair trade, because the party with more information has a clear advantage. When buyers and sellers have different information about the goods or services being sold, whichever party knows more can also dictate the outcome of the transaction. You don't want to lose when playing this game; make good decisions and you will sleep well, save money, and avoid countless headaches.

Do your research.

Hunches have value, but betting on hunches have cost me plenty, even when I was operating in circumstances that were familiar. Hunches can work, but you will need a larger cushion if you fall, and a lot of experience to do well with hunches.

Warren Buffet started investing without the internet. Information was not at his fingertips and the search for information was far more difficult and time-consuming. Reading financial reports and trusting company executives was more challenging and burdensome.

One of Warren Buffett's ground rules is explained; in the 2016 HBO documentary, Becoming Warren Buffet, Buffet himself explains it this way:

"I can look at a thousand different companies and I don't have to be right on every one of them, or even 50 of them. So, I can pick the ball I want to hit. The trick in investing is just to sit there and watch pitch after pitch go by and wait for the one right in your sweet spot. And the people who are yelling 'swing, you bum,' ignore them."

Knowing what you know increases the probability of your suppositions, theories, and hunches being accurate; you can start strong and decide with confidence. You would not need to be right about every decision if you were Warren Buffet; perhaps you have a cushion and don't need to be right. When you are an expert and you can afford to relax, because you're not going to take wild aim, you stand a good chance of hitting the target.

With this said, don't forget to do your due diligence on the company and the individuals who run it. For almost every one of us, liking the way the ball is thrown cannot be the only reason to swing at it.

Making decisions that rely on other peoples' performance will require additional risk assessment.

When you depend on another person or a groups' performance *and can fail based on no fault of your own,* you are then ready to make not one, but two, decisions. The first decision is simply to determine if your 'partner' or dependent entity is worthy of trust. Too often we are asked to trust others who haven't had the opportunity to earn the trust they seek. Deciding who to trust is clearly your responsibility.

We need to remember that reputations can be altered; some reputations can be cleared online, and some reputations may suffer unfair complaints. We are in an era of reviews and ratings. The larger the sample size, the more likely to see a generally true view or probable expectation of performance.

Here is a major confession; I would never want you to make my mistake. I was 'had' by a con man. Please understand that I choose not to share names regarding this matter.

My husband and I had an investment property in beautiful Sedona, Arizona. When we bought it, we knew that remodeling was absolutely necessary and that certain maintenance issues were deferred and overdue. We hired a licensed contractor to correct some issues that could have been disastrous, and they also upgraded some worn flooring and a kitchen that was both shabby and damaged. Five years later, we realized that it was necessary to contract more work on this home. We decided to do a major remodel that would have handled two important goals; we could have more bedrooms and bathrooms and rent the house as a better value, and it would be the type of home we could enjoy when we decided to retire.

At that time, water damage alerted us that repairs were imperative, so we decided to use the dry season in Arizona to get this remodel finished. In most regions of Arizona, it is pretty certain that it doesn't rain from April until late July. August is a notorious month for rain; it is referred to as monsoon season. I used the winter to look for contractors and draw up plans for this necessary remodel. We hired a General Contractor that was licensed and held a Better Business Bureau A+ rating, and we had confidence in him. After he hired an unlicensed contractor to do grading and drainage and told me it was legal to do so, I checked the laws and found out that he could not legally do so. On top of this, he decided to ask for more money for roofing. We had a signed contract and we felt he had no right to ask for more money. With these issues occurring, we felt no way to move forward, so I told him that we were better off parting ways. We had issues with reconciling the money we had already paid, but the clock was ticking, and the monsoons were eminent, so I found another licensed General Contractor to carry out the plans.

I checked the license of the contractor to be certain that they had no complaints. They looked very clean and my husband and I felt very comfortable with their new foreman. We adored him and wanted him to do work in other properties when he finished this remodel. Little did we know he had been in and out of prison for defrauding many homeowners, and he was a very formidable con man.

After he had started the tear-out and rebuild on the house, we noticed many issues which were alarming, but possibly the most stressful occurrence was the demand for more money than was agreed to, in the contract. We didn't have any signed change orders or expectations of upgrades. This was very slow to reconcile and before long, monsoons came, and we were in big trouble without a roof, and a deck that was built without the engineered slant for drainage.

To make a long story short, this did not end well. Had we simply checked the name of the foreman using an Internet search, his numerous prison records would have popped up in a split second, and this outrageous experience could have been avoided.

I cannot stress enough that research is necessary to make good decisions. Don't be in a hurry. I had no idea what kind of risk we were accepting. I learned many lessons that were very painful; just writing a legal contract and paying the money as agreed, did not create the space for my remodel to be successful. My story is not unique; there are countless similar stories. After my experience, I no longer allow people to work on my property without seeing their worker's compensation insurance and knowing the credentials of every sub-contractor that steps onto my property. There is much more to this type of transaction but signing lien releases with every check I pay is an extra step to be certain that issues don't come back to haunt me.

I did my best at the time, but if I can tell you something to illustrate how important details are when making a decision, you can use my experience to your advantage. You don't need to re-invent the wheel, and you don't have to step in the same puddles others have.

I would urge you not to fear, but instead to keep your eye on the ball. Don't get lazy and trust people that haven't earned your trust. As you will see in future chapters, you cannot be rushed. The best way to predict the future behavior of a person is to note and monitor their past behavior. When I see an individual with the potential to trust, but not the time to witness their performance history, I will start slow with small tasks and watch their performance. When small tasks are completed, I can add larger tasks to see how they handle larger duties. After a while, performance is assumedly predictable. If you are running out of time, make certain to notice absolutely everything about this person or this company. Whatever you do, do not justify excuses for little things that did not go well. Don't try to be overly-understanding or prematurely-forgiving when they said something strange or did something that wasn't to your liking. The best course is to believe it is a needed sign for you to consider seriously.

Perhaps your decision is personal, not a business dilemma. For example, a possible mate appears in your life, and you seem to have mutual attraction. It's normal to want to believe that this person is the answer to your search. It is typical (but foolish) to believe that a person that you hardly know will not harm you and that their heart is in the right place. (Remember my con man.) I believe people need to be observed for 90 days, and no sign can be ignored. Anyone can behave well for a short amount of time but watch this person consistently for a few months and you will see things that will become recurring themes. Being too desperate will get you into trouble. I don't want to rely on shock value to convince my readers that it isn't wise to be alone with or go to bed with someone you hardly know. I certainly know people that have had their watches and jewelry stolen in such circumstances when they want to take an affectionate relationship to the next level. The truth is, you are risking your life in such a situation, and that makes no sense at all. Always remember, **trust is earned**.

Reputations can be scrubbed and manipulated online. Be aware when you see less than 10 reviews. There is actual, earned trust in an online seller who delivers 99.5% of the time and has very high ratings when the ratings or reviews for this business are tabulated with hundreds or thousands of reviews. You want your purchase to be as advertised and on time, and it is unlikely a seller with these many reviews will fail. Scientifically, a larger sample size for any experiment will have more credible findings. When accurate results matter, large sample sizes will yield more data and give a better range of possible outcomes.

Those organizations and websites that offer buyers information about companies are often not a fully reliable source of reputation data. By joining (paying for membership) in the Better Business Bureau, reviewed companies have an advantage over consumers, and they pay for it in dollars. When I leave a review, I am trying to help people I may never know that could have a bad experience, and certainly, I also want to appreciate companies that have been very helpful to me. When a company opts to pay the rating organization, they will have the advantage over the consumer. Complaints and poor results may not be handled objectively. Many online reputations and fact checking sites are no better than the inclinations of the powers that operate them. Expand your search for information and do not rely on one source.

There is a repetitive theme in this book: don't miss it. **Being lazy will not yield your best outcome**. If your results are important, do not take the short cuts. You can really experience terrible, unexpected consequences by not investing energy and effort.

Relying on the performance of others will always be tricky. It is also true that other people can make mistakes, even without malice, and your awareness can save you grief. We must always watch for signs. Entering a contract is a decision, but you must also decide to be aware and manage the situation. I certainly suffered from information asymmetry. Anyone with a search engine could have known I was dealing with a sociopathic foreman who enjoyed harming people and made a game out of this. The licensed General Contractor who hired him also knew and benefitted by his excellent 'salesmanship.' Remember, *we felt that this con man was a joy to work with*...until it was too late.

There are con artists and scammers everywhere, and they rely on information asymmetry to gain the superior position in the deal. When one lacks information, look for context. All the tools are available in this day and age to make better decisions. It's so typical for people to happily move ahead with decisions with so little context, on a hunch or a feeling. Without solid information, people love to form opinions from headlines and tweets, just regurgitating what others with differing points of reference might want to post for their advantage, without your needs directing their intentions. People are misled every minute of the day, and one of the most powerless things we can do is to repeat, without thinking or researching others' points of view. We often lack necessary research to choose what is best. Snake oil is peddled everywhere in all walks of life. Schemers have been around for a long time, but the internet has certainly made it more difficult for them to survive. The wisest people can check unlikely resources to find other leads to the truth about anything that they find important to know or to find. Information is now virtually free, so laziness is foolishness. Don't allow other people to think for you; their intentions may not be pure. When your search isn't offering the necessary information, 'follow the money' and you will see the true story behind the question. Ideas are peddled by those who gain quietly in the background.

I cannot stress enough that we all must notice how people behave and take their promises with a grain of salt. If you want to know what someone will do, watch their patterns over time; this will be the best indicator.

Avoid using outdated answers in a changing world. Interim agreement isn't fact, it just illustrates how large groups of people believe, similar to general consensus, and most of them did not do any research or think for themselves. Mindlessly, people take the opinions of others and call them their own. This is not the type of advanced thinking we need in an advancing world. Outdated information is commonly used for these beliefs and choosing not to think is dangerous. Your beliefs are sacred; they determine your modus operandi and can send you in the wrong direction. Mind and recheck your belief system so that it serves you and takes you to the places you want to go. Your beliefs must align with your principles. If not, you will not enjoy your outcome.

My dad always warned me, as a child, "The masses are asses." Thank you, Dad. People choose to invest when it's already too late to gain and the prices are high. The great investors buy when there is blood in the streets, but this does not feel safe until you have lived through enough cycles to predict cycles somewhat reliably.

U.S. President Andrew Jackson said, "Mere precedent is a dangerous source of authority." This is the same as doing something repeatedly, in a pattern. This is not like rolling dice; we are not referring to mathematical probabilities. Calculate the factual and timely data. Please don't allow yourself to be lazy by trying to skip this step.

I have the ability to count calories in food without weighing portions. I have done it so many times, I can eyeball it. There is no risk when I do this, and I save time with the same results. Some people have exponential success without the kind of financial research we would need to do before going forward with a deal. Learning quickly is a fallacy.

On the Spiritual Level, when you are 'in the zone" one simply knows what they know, effortlessly. In the Introduction of this book, I mentioned my Karate Grandmaster's Five Level Method. The Academic Level, backed with other distinctions, such as the Psychological Level will allow you to know what you know, becoming an expert.

I suppose that when you are on Buffett's level, with his vast experience, it can be expensive not to take a risk when it feels right.

On the opposite plane, many people never learn from mistakes and do the same thing over and over. It's time to **wake up**.

"There is nothing that is a more certain sign of insanity than to do the same thing over and over and expect the results to be different."

~ Albert Einstein

The Benefits of Calculating Risk

You will know what you have risked. You will learn which rewards you stand to gain. Estimating these factors or being absolutely on target will inspire you to achieve. It may also allow you to sleep well if you are committed and you can stay true to your decision. I am claiming that it is better to know your risks and take risks with the benefit of peace of mind.

The Implementation

Overcome the disadvantage of information asymmetry by searching for the necessary back story. Don't calculate this 'fast and dirty' in your head. You can only juggle a little information without organizing the data on a screen or paper; you may get sophisticated by creating a spreadsheet. This is a game of weighing outcomes. You must have a minimum of two columns and create lists for possible choices. If your calculations are mathematical, you will compute your numbers for what you are risking and what you stand to gain. Allow these things to resonate and don't make a decision without proper research. Use facts only, not opinions. Also remember, trust is earned.

The objective point of view is needed here and not to be confused with the next step regarding objectives; this is a contextual dissimilarity.

Objective thinking is not influenced by personal feelings or opinions when considering facts. This thinking is neutral, unbiased and unprejudiced. It is fair-minded, even-handed and uninterested to take sides. Juries are intended to be impartial or objective; the blindfold on the Lady of Justice relies upon this objectivity.

The Cost of NOT Calculating Risks

It's certainly practical to know what you have to lose. Would you go to a casino and pay no attention to what you are betting? We need to give some strong and serious thought to the decisions we make and the decisions we delay making. There are costs to not choosing, so let's not take that lightly either.

My father reminded me repeatedly, when you **assume,** *you make an* **ass** *out of* **you** *and* **me.**

WE NEED TO GIVE SOME STRONG AND SERIOUS THOUGHT TO THE DECISIONS WE MAKE AND THE DECISIONS WE DELAY MAKING. THERE ARE ALSO COSTS TO NOT CHOOSING.

STEP #5
Applying Objectives
will Save You

When one makes decisions and lives by objectives that are positive for oneself as well as others, it removes much potential discomfort from the outcome of that decision. When we allow the agendas of others to sway us, we can be drawn off target from our own intentions. Pulled in a direction that is less important, not worth the time, or even detrimental.

When we disregard our values, principles, and objectives, we risk failure. We are likely to quit before completion when our subconscious mind believes it is doing us a favor by abandoning something that isn't meaningful or is likely to be out of the scope of our ideals and beliefs.

Being fully conscious of what we are doing and what we are creating will aid us in our use of objectives. Principles and values are also aligned with corresponding decisions and implementation.

This is a very direct chapter that has clear-cut instructions for making decisions. Most thoughtful processes are more personal or internal for the individual. Naturally, every person has their own ideals, and these concepts affirm their value as a being, otherwise these objectives must be discarded. You will find some hard and true rules in this chapter that are to be followed by everyone in all circumstances, making this step unique. These objectives will be described fully in this chapter, so you can understand when and how they apply. **These objectives alone can bring you instantly to a "yes" or "no" when making a decision in many circumstances where these objectives apply.**

Objectives are strategies or implementation steps to achieve the chosen outcomes. Unlike goals, objectives are measurable, but they are not goals. Objectives are specific, and they are meant to be lifelong, without a completion date. They will explain details to align with goals and add structure when making decisions.

> *"The pleasure principle long persists, however, as the method of working employed by the sexual instincts, which are so hard to 'educate', and, starting from those instincts, or in the ego itself, it often succeeds in overcoming the reality principle, to the detriment of the organism as a whole."*
>
> ~ Sigmund Freud

Our first objective is to control the ego. Sigmund Freud is known for his studies of the psyche, including the Id, Ego, and Superego. Freud said that children are completely egoistic. They feel their needs intensely and strive ruthlessly to satisfy them. This is quite self-serving and immature. As we discuss the ego, we will need to remember that the ego exists not for the good of mankind, but to make a weak attempt to preserve self-esteem. I can assure you that people with high self-esteem and without worthiness issues will not need to protect their ego. They would not give the ego credence if they understood it. For readers who believe in God, I like to use this acronym for EGO--- Edging God Out. The ego is self-centered and does not serve our highest good. It doesn't even give us lasting happiness when it is served. There is no meaningful reward in regarding the ego. Very often it does not help us to become financially wealthy. It often impairs our earning potential by pushing us into poor decisions, made for the wrong reasons. Ego also frequently causes bad choices in relationships where neither party is well-served. Both people are likely to be damaged by a relationship that exists to fuel the ego. This may all seem surprising because people are led to believe that the ego is somehow good for self-preservation. The part of the self that it preserves is selfish and unproductive.

Conversely, it is true that many rich people have huge egos. I propose that the empires they created would have been grander in size and importance if they disregarded their egos. Please do not compare 'branding' to the ego. Because the ego never helps others, the conscious equivalent does not add up to anything important to society. In other words, there is no marketable value for decisions driven by the ego. There is nothing spiritually divine that results from a decision made with the ego. You are not your ego.

Your ego is your image of yourself, conscious or subconscious, and it strives for validation and approval. It is only a social mask, and it might as well be a mask because it lives in fear, wanting to control people and circumstances for more validation of its importance.

Any decision made for reasons of the ego are the wrong decisions. When we make choices to flatter ourselves, rather than to create win-win situations, we can be sure that this behavior is detrimental. Cajoling and self-praise are simply worthless, but self-love is desirable. Self-love comes from self- actualization as well as jobs well done that improve conditions for humanity or the planet. Self-love also comes from God. Since God unconditionally loves each of us, it is arrogant to disagree with God. If God knows we are worth love, then we must learn that we are worthy of it for ourselves. Loving ourselves unquestionably is a requirement to transcend the ego. Self-love and the ego are not the same. Those who make decisions in consult with their egos are not self-loving. They are self-doubting and employing a defense mechanism. If you are trying to prove that you are good, then you really don't believe that you are good. Your own self-worth is not in your grasp when driven by ego. It is rather at the mercy of circumstances.

I do not suggest that you do not serve yourself with your decisions. I do suggest that win-win decisions and situations are valuable. Mutually beneficial interactions with others will lead you toward self-love, self-respect, and they will direct you to self-actualization, which is the highest lifelong goal we can attain. When we have hit the pinnacle of being fulfilled, we have achieved it by doing much to help others. We have also successfully served our own relationships and finances. Self-actualized people feel rewarded. We know that life is a gift because we feel aligned with the Universe. Making the right decisions for you, independent of defending your ego will lead you directly toward self-actualization. Conscious, intentional decisions regarding how you spend your time, manage your goals, and fulfill your accomplishments will determine how and when you reach self- actualization. The empowered and exhilarated feelings that self-actualized people enjoy are lasting, not fleeting like buying a new car. You may feel good when you get a new car, but if you do it for your ego, that feeling will not fill you with joy. There will be some accompanying doubt and you will look for the next "fix" to feed the ego. This explains why the malls are crowded every weekend by people who are looking for "stuff" to feel good or reward their lives. There is nothing you can buy to fill you with infinite joy. It is likely that finding and purchasing the perfect shirt will leave you soon empty, like the old Chinese food analogy: *You will be hungry again an hour later.* Joy and self-love are inside you, and if you don't have it, seek your purpose in life, and fulfill it with dignity, passion, and integrity. You will then make great decisions because your objectives are serving your universally-directed purpose instead of feeding the ego. Your purpose is the key to your happiness and no one can tell you what your purpose is. It is in your soul, like a blueprint. Working with your purpose in mind will help you to maintain a path of productivity, good relationships, high self-esteem, and very likely financial wealth that stems directly or indirectly from your accomplishments.

In my travels, I found this in a book in my hotel nightstand:

To Our Guests

In ancient times, there was a prayer for "The Stranger within our gates." It continues, "Because this hotel is a human institution to serve people, and not solely a money-making organization, we hope that God will grant you peace and rest while you are under our roof," and it continues in an elegant manner. This is a prime example of purpose and objectives. I can't be sure that all of those employed by the hotel understand this mission, but the owner is clear about it, and as he succeeds in giving people peace and rest under his roof, he enjoys his own self-actualization and financial rewards. He is charitable, allowing those who think his rates are expensive to know that he gives and shares his fortune. This good will is passed down, again comforting his guests. Basically, we are here not only to serve ourselves, but when we serve others as well, we succeed. Successful people achieve success not because of how they glorify themselves; their success is due to the aid they give to others, expressed with appreciation.

To clarify "decisions made by the ego" I submit to you a few examples:

- Buying a grand home (or car, or clothing, etc.) that one cannot really afford

- Deciding not to act to help others in order to avoid being judged harshly.

- Self-aggrandizement with public self-praise

- Starting a business that helps no one, has no value, and promotes the self

- Breaking laws or hurting others to simplify one's life or reduce one's obligations

- Arrogant behavior

- Unrealistically demanding behavior

- Spending time in an unproductive manner that flatters the self and is hurtful to someone else

- Wasting someone's time to get attention, or what psychologists call 'mirroring' i.e. dating people that one may not care about, just for entertainment value

- Having babies with no plan for their welfare or future

- Taking harmful and/or illegal steroids to body build or increase musculature or performance

- Smoking cigarettes to control one's weight

- Persisting with anorexia or bulimia as a mechanism to preserve or enhance the self-image

This may give you an idea of how the ego works in different areas of life. Basic psychology will teach you about the ego if you wish to seek more information. It is important to remember for our purposes, that the ego can cause us to make choices that are not in our best interest. The ego limits a person because it is protecting itself. Your ego is your enemy; it is not to be confused with self-respect. Living by high principles and objectives will bring forth greater results in every aspect of your life, rather than acting to protect your ego.

"Nothing truly valuable arises from ambition or from a mere sense of duty."

~ Albert Einstein

Coincidentally, beyond principled living, there are three other objectives that I recommend. These happen to be the foundational directives of certified hypnotherapists. These are appropriate and mature 'protectors.'

Patients are generally unaware of these ethical directives that pave the way for trust and healing.

The first of these three objectives is preservation of the self. Notice that this regards the health of one's body and entire life. It has nothing to do with the ego.

In the world of hypnosis, most reasons to seek treatment are to stop smoking or overeating, to reduce physical pain, to control anxiety or anger, or to enhance self-esteem. There are many other treatments that are not mentioned, but please notice that this short list is an inventory of health and life enhancements. We can all enrich our lives with better health, both mentally and physically. It is also common for a hypnosis patient to wish to stop procrastinating, so he or she can earn more money or get organized. Prosperity and healthy finances can improve other aspects of one's life.

Every time a decision is made, the choice between avoiding pain and gaining pleasure is assessed. Caring for our mental or physical health may conflict, or at least complicate this issue.

Smoking a cigarette is a prime example of gaining pleasure and/or avoiding pain. Obviously, preserving the self complicates the issue because there is no reason to smoke where one's health is concerned. Smoking has been proven to cause cancer and emphysema. I think we are crystal clear regarding this. In addition, we all know that addictions ought to be treated.

Addiction is recognizably present when we cannot keep our word due to the addiction. We may stumble, awaken, and strive for a life of freedom, uncontrolled by substances or addictive thoughts.

What would you do if someone pointed a gun at you and asked for your money and your jewelry? If you were making a choice to preserve yourself, you would likely surrender the money and jewelry, knowing that these possessions can be replaced. Most likely you would not be killed, and you would preserve yourself. Very few people could defeat an armed robber, so this would be an appropriate decision for almost everyone.

The second objective to live by is preservation of others, and the third is preservation of the planet. Many people have misconceptions of hypnosis because they have seen a movie or TV show in which a person was hypnotized to kill or harm someone else. Please understand this as an absolute fact: during hypnosis or post-hypnosis, there is NO risk that someone will do ANYTHING that they would not do in a fully conscious state. A non-murderer will not murder. The same goes for rape, shoplifting, or acting out in any way. An introverted person will not get up on stage, dance around and cluck like a chicken under hypnosis, unless they would do it 'awake.' Hypnosis first relaxes and next it 'suggests' the subconscious mind, offering an invitation to do it.

Preservation of others may bring forth questions, such as the question of competition. If I open a store that sells the same thing as the store 300 feet away, am I hurting that store? There is a universal rule here— competition does not apply. Competition is good for everyone. It gives customers more selection, better pricing, and hopefully, better service. Much of competition in theory isn't competitive at all. A consumer will be drawn to the source that is best for him or her. Consumers are so different; they will choose different stores due to their own preferences. Have you ever seen a Taco Bell open hundreds of feet from a McDonalds? Very often a Burger King will move in nearby as well. Not only is this good for consumers, because it brings variety and choices forth, but all will be served as more consumers looking for food will be drawn to that area of town. A "hub" is formed and all of the restaurants can feed off of each other's business. In addition, spiritually inclined people don't believe in competition. This is an advanced belief for most people, but knowing how different individuals are, whether they are a supplier or a consumer, there just isn't much competition in actuality. Suppliers also evolve into specialties that are advantageous to both buyers and sellers. Compatible living, with the preservation of others does not exclude competition, so do your market analysis and open your business as you see fit. You may actually help your seeming competitor, and they may help you.

Self-defense may harm an attacker but preserve the self or others. If an intruder enters your home with the intent to harm or kill you or your family, you have the legal and moral right to defend your family. Acquiescing to an uninvited intruder is foolish and could cost you a spouse or a child, or potentially your own life. Enough said. I say, a life worth having is a life worth preserving.

I believe that preservation of others includes *not* smoking. There is much documentation and proof that nonsmokers have died from exposure to secondhand smoke. Even if someone prefers not to breathe the smoke from your cigarette, that right to smell clean air deserves preservation. Smokers are harming others by smoking. Having a no smoking section in a restaurant is as ridiculous as having a no peeing section in a swimming pool. If the tobacco lobby in the U.S. wasn't so well-funded and powerful, smoking would certainly be illegal. The lost jobs of this industry could be shifted to the care of people instead of their destruction.

There are many controversial behaviors that you must eventually take to heart. Some people think drugs make life better or reduce pain, however there are too many cases where those under the influence have harmed others. The country of Singapore has a no tolerance policy for drugs. They allow drinking alcohol but as you arrive into Singapore, they hand out a warning with customs documents that say that you will be executed for bringing drugs into Singapore. Singapore has a very productive society where almost 90% of people own their own homes and work. Their crime rate is extremely low, almost non-existent, so when you research drug-related crime in other countries, please notice that drugs are a large element in overall crime statistics.

Many life-altering decisions fall into this category or rule. Abortion may seemingly preserve the self by avoiding inconvenience, but it will destroy the potential of a human life. It is not my mission to judge others; I believe God is the judge. Abortion is an excellent example because it is such a meaningful decision with huge impact. Speaking as a psychologist, much guilt has arisen in therapy sessions over abortion, and admittedly, many women have confessed to me that they made a wrong choice because it was so mentally painful before, during, and after the procedure. A woman can understandably decide not to give birth to a rapist's child, but forgetting to use birth control is simply irresponsible. Obviously, most abortions in the U.S. are the result of careless behavior. As human beings, we need to closely examine this and make better choices, especially before the act. In metaphysics, it is said, there is no right or wrong, only consequences; this is a sure way to take the spiritual path and not judge others. One hundred years into the future, is it possible that all of humanity may look back and judge us, certain that this practice was barbaric?

A possible decision may be adoption. There are many people who wish to raise a child and can't afford the exorbitant cost and risk to adopt one from overseas. Many women could choose to turn a negative into a positive with a decision to give an unwanted child up for adoption at birth. Responsible parents could adopt healthy babies since the demand is larger than the supply in America. There is a growing issue of infertility in the U.S. due to many factors. Not having children would be a responsible decision for most people without enough time or know-how to raise children. In so many ways, the self's goal of gaining pleasure and avoiding pain directly conflicts with the objective to preserve others. Having heard both sides of the argument, you will learn in the next step about 'justifying behavior' versus mindfulness. This is an immense decision, personal and complicated. Making good, appropriate decisions before reaching a crossroads will absolutely avoid pain and gain pleasure, which is the purpose of this book.

Beyond the self and others, apply these rules to our Earth. Choosing to litter instead of finding a trash can is selfish, as is all pollution. We can all financially afford to find a garbage can, so this is not an excuse. When you can see that others suffer from your decision on this level, you must reconsider such actions. Recycling of goods such as paper, glass, and metals is a good example of the preservation of the planet, of others, and of oneself— everyone wins. We can do our best with preservation of the resources we can financially afford, and strive to do better in the future. My husband and I usually drive our Priuses and live in our homes that are powered by solar energy. This also allows us to give back to the grid and our neighbors. Most people cannot afford the cost of these blessings, so when it becomes affordable, more will be able to do it. We must all live within our means and strive to upgrade for humanity as soon as it becomes possible.

When you see a sweater or any clothing in your closet that you are not using, give it to someone who is in need. Quietly celebrate your generosity with that warm-hearted feeling. Never waste resources that can be better utilized. Be grateful that you get to serve others.

As I sit and write, Paris is burning. Human suffering exists. The European middle class cannot financially afford the huge taxes that are imposed in many countries; they are experiencing dangerous demonstrations. Perhaps the government must seek better and more affordable solutions to serve our planet. As governments and as individuals, we must live within our means and strive for a better world and a better life. No one said it isn't complicated; scientists will be busy.

Animals may need protection from potential extinction, while termites eating your home, may need to be destroyed. Buddhists may decide to give the termite-infested home to the termites and buy another home since this resonates with their values and belief system. The bank may then decide to repossess and re-sell that home, and a buyer may hire an exterminator to eradicate the termites. Decisions have personal complexity. What's right for some may not be so for others, but through it all, some universal truths can be applied.

Life is fragile. That's why scientists of different disciplines are hired so we might maximize our existence without damaging our planet. Alternative fuels, solar power, and other new technologies that may help to preserve this planet are worthy, practical, and admirable endeavors. Until we can make a full conversion to such power sources, we must choose to turn off lights, use less air-conditioning, and use timers to lower bills and conserve the planet's resources. Wasting *anything* is irresponsible behavior that we can change.

As a single member of this planet's population, each of our choices will actually affect many others. My aim is to inspire every reader to think before they act, and to be aligned with their goals, the rights of others, and the needs of the planet. Conscientious living may seem initially inconvenient but is important. We may not always be capable of living up to this standard, but we must strive to do so as often as we can. In the meantime, my aim is not to judge the occasions when we fall short of the goal, but instead build each of us back up.

With this said, once you think you know everything, you know nothing. This is the wisdom of the Buddha that will apply universally forever. Know what you know, but pay attention to changing trends and new forces that can interrupt the changing environment.

The Benefits of These Objectives

When a person lives by objectives that are positive for the self, others, and the planet, it removes the struggle from the outcome of the decision. Feeling aligned with others allows us to sleep well at night, knowing that we carefully considered our options and we made the best decision for all at the time. If in the end, the decision then results in a bad outcome, we can live peacefully with it, understanding that despite all of these principles, we are fallible, human, and we all make mistakes. By formulating our decisions with this degree of conviction we will enjoy the fruits of compassion more often and the peace of acceptance when we turn out to be wrong.

Healing addictions is another way to be free and live a healthier life; this is true for the self, others and the world.

The Implementation

If you are challenged by any objectives in this chapter, you may seek help, whether you choose free assistance or you choose to pay a professional. Live free from addiction and watch your entire life bloom into your most wonderful and abundant desires. Do unto others as you would have them do unto you. Stop littering, start recycling, and conserve energy and resources whenever applicable. Be part of the solution in every possible situation instead of part of the problem.

The Cost of Living without these Objectives

Your self-esteem will rise when you live with higher consciousness. Making decisions from a more responsible and conscious place will reduce the number of conflicted decisions and mistakes that will confront you in the future. A simple act such as littering will affect the planet, others and also yourself. It is time for higher consciousness to prevail. *If you throw litter on the street, does it make your self-esteem increase or decrease? These answers are within you.*

Objectives build valuable people in society and in the world. Children can be raised by these objectives. By solving problems instead of generating them, we spark a powerful shift in the world.

BY SOLVING PROBLEMS INSTEAD OF GENERATING THEM, WE SPARK A POWERFUL SHIFT IN THE WORLD.

As I conclude this chapter, I reiterate that every decision you make, big or small, has the power to influence others and potentially the world.

Economists are plagued with unintended consequences. We must also consider that unintended consequences are quite likely. There is a domino effect, like a ripple in the ocean that is created by your actions. Following these objectives may simplify your decision and amplify your accuracy. With so much to consider, some decisions will be more difficult to make, and they may take more time. I think part of my goal is to teach people to slow down in their decision-making process. An appropriate amount of time taken to properly consider decisions will be rewarded in the long term by making more of them correctly.

**STEP #6
The Gift of Intuition
and How to Use It**

What does your gut say? When you identify a question that needs an answer, what is the validity of your first inclination? The value of the intuition of others who aren't involved may not be helpful to you, however it is extremely important to know when your intuition rules.

I warned you not to rely solely on your hunch or others' thoughts and opinions. There is a place for using your own intuition, but please don't discount the other steps and valuable research.

So often people will suppress that gut feeling. The hunch that "reasons" are more important than intuition is very prevalent. Generally, people believe that following the gut is a little primitive. Justification seems less archaic to most folks. This assumption is incorrect. Intuition is valuable, and justification is counterproductive. We can take a look at decision-making through justification. We will examine the inclinations, costs, and pay-offs of this mode of decision-making.

We often justify because it makes us feel good about our choices or seeming losses. This is because we validate ourselves as being right. Cognitive dissonance offers us a way to turn discomfort into "reasons" and justification. The reasons we justify appear valuable, but if we could calculate the costs, maybe our rationalizations, intended meanings, or our defenses would look far less attractive.

Justification stems from the ego. Intuition comes from mindfulness.

Justifying the situation is only another way of being self-righteous or "being right." Many people get satisfaction from believing they are right, but we know we can't read minds, guess their reasons, or whatever they choose to do to gain pleasure or avoid pain. We can only be sure of the thoughts in our own heads. Judging others, predicting others' behavior, or contemplating others' thoughts is a waste of time. Trying to guess others' intentions takes away from where we really need to focus. It's best to aim for **yourself and your desired outcome**. I am not saying that repercussions that affect others are not important. I am saying **think for yourself**. Go back and focus on what the correct decision could mean to you. What is at stake for you?

We lose our own self-expression and desired direction when we justify a situation to avoid looking silly. For example, when you love someone who has hurt you, you might benefit from telling him or her you love them but you're hurt. We lose our chance to clear up a situation or misunderstanding when we decide others are a lost cause by validating a personal loss as 'being right.' *I would certainly rather be happy than right, wouldn't you? I also value completion over allowing something to haunt my mind in the future.* Often people will apologize when they find they have been hurtful. Stay open rather than justify and give the other party a chance to care. They may also explain their intentions. We could save the time spent second-guessing them. We will have a better life and better results when we look for the win-win and give it a chance. If happy endings are not in the cards, others will not feel the need to hold onto hate for us when we are vulnerable and open our hearts. Clearing the air has value. Self-expression is too powerful to sacrifice. Most small children don't have self-expression. Therefore, they can't create deep relationships. they are merely dependents. Evolved people choose not to justify.

We cannot guess what someone else is thinking. People in general are so busy playing guessing games. They are deterred from asking a simple question when another being is involved. You may look more foolish guessing wrong than asking out loud. There is value in being straightforward rather than avoiding games or trying to predict others' actions. The best thing we can do is much simpler.

Pertaining to the situation, just ask (for example), "Would you like to get together?" or "Would you like to do business together?" Just try it. If the answer is no, just thank them for their honesty, and move on to the next opportunity. In a case where they say no and mean yes, it is still better to move on, because it isn't worth dealing with people's hidden agendas and games. The time that is wasted won't be returned to us. We are just investing time to learn a lesson that might already be clear.

So far, we know that justifying costs us love and self-expression; this is also true in a purposeful business world. When the pay-off is only smug satisfaction, we are left empty. For that moment we were avoiding pain and gaining pleasure by invalidating someone else. It also costs us our vitality, health, and fulfillment.

Being human and having a brain can drive us crazy. We can pull cheap tricks on ourselves such as substantiating ourselves by invalidating others. Thereby we lose happiness, intimacy and relationships. Such is the case when we make decisions about others by justifying their behavior.

Human weakness can lead to cognitive dissonance. Be reassured, knowing our minds are capable of evolving. We can find comfort knowing that passion and integrity are stronger than our pay-offs of dominating and nullifying others.

We must stay focused on our passions and possibilities. This is where our happiness lies. If we can keep our energy on the big picture, little battles will diminish. *Do you see how second-guessing and justification can cause an invalid detour to making a good decision?* Now we can move on to why our own intuition is a great tool.

The answers you seek are truly within you, and they are not afterthoughts like justification. You will find your gut speaks to you first, which is indeed convenient. Please note that. The biggest obstacle would be information asymmetry. You may need to follow up with specifics to make a complete decision. However, **your intuition is the best tool you have for general, everyday decisions.** The only way to use your intuition to serve yourself, others, and anything that dominos from a decision, is to trust yourself. When we feel we are aligned with goodness, love, wisdom, prosperity, and more spiritual qualities, this is easy. Too many people are not that far evolved. Let's discuss aligning with all of the good qualities one could hope to express.

The first thing we must know is that "nice" is not a spiritual quality. Compassion is. Love is. Generosity is. There are more qualities, however, "nice" is not a spiritual quality. *Being nice is* being a doormat. *Do you like being stepped on?* Because this is often how you will feel when you make your decisions in order to be nice to someone. Aim toward win-wins and compromises instead of trying to be nice. We think we have to be nice. **If you are generous, wise, and compassionate, *nice* need not enter the picture.** Being nice can be damaging to your own situation. All decisions ought to make you feel good and aligned with spiritual qualities and goodness. We need not say to ourselves, "Oh, boy. I hope I didn't get myself into something painful or detrimental." That happens when we justify by being nice and then the intuition chimes in and says, "I think that was an error."

There is absolutely nothing gained by allowing yourself to be a doormat. Have a reason to say "yes", and a principle behind every "no." If your son or daughter needs punishment, don't allow being loving to spoil the child and spare the punishment. Loving is not a 'doormat condition'. Being a parent is not a time for being nice and taking the low road to make friends with your kids. It is far more important to hold your ground and to exercise 'tough love' whenever applicable. Don't be a doormat or you will be disrespected now and in the future. This is also true with dogs. Dogs don't want to be the master. Many think they want to run the house and be the 'alpha,' but a happy dog is a dog that knows its place and obeys. Obeying can save a dog's life. Take control over that which you are responsible. Accountability is certainly an important and prominent spiritual quality.

Making decisions that are win-wins will not be painful. Since this is what we are striving toward, let's be good to ourselves, not self-sabotaging. Get it?

Getting back to aligning with divine qualities, how can we achieve this? The problems that arise from the old, poor decisions of the past are the major cause of feeling unaligned with spiritual qualities and principles right now. The truth is, each and every one of us is holding every spiritual quality inside, even if these qualities are a bit rusty. We make the choice, moment-by-moment to be loving, generous, compassionate, honest, or to use any other spiritual feature we possess. The qualities of consistency and accountability allow us to shine and show our value to the world.

Recognize that we are not only physical beings, but also spiritual and divine beings having a physical incarnation. When we accept this as Truth, we walk a different walk and talk a different talk. It is easier to have patience with others. It is easier to share. It is a simple task to smile at another being when we recognize them as another divine being. As I said in the introduction of this book, spirituality is the belief that we are all connected. When we recognize this invisible association that we have with others and the planet, we make better choices. This is natural and guaranteed. It is infinite in nature.

You will want to choose to conduct yourself as an example of these behaviors, and you will wish for those with whom you interact, to return these spiritual gestures. If you didn't love your children, you would not care what they do. If you want your kids to grow up as responsible adults, discipline is needed. Dealing with adults is similar yet different. You can respectfully tell other adults when you don't agree with them, just do it in a more mature and loving way. You would not treat anyone with disrespect if you understood that they are made out of the same stuff you are. This is an unrealized concept for most human beings. In times of difference, recognizing underlying similarities will lead to a good decision or faster solution.

When you accept that you are just as deserving of good as anyone else, you can begin to trust your intuition. Those who are less confident in their goodness reach for justification, expressed by the ego. Those with high self-esteem, that are certain their existence will make the world better can use intuition with greater ease. Intuition will grace your process; it's beneficial in making decisions.

For some, intuition sounds feminine. For others intuition sounds spiritual. As a matter of fact, intuition is for everyone and within everyone. Sometimes intuition will try so strongly and profoundly to interrupt us, we receive it like a thunderclap. Most of the time, it goes unnoticed and unheard.

I previously mentioned that I have interviewed over 20,000 single people in the United States regarding their past marriages and relationships. I also have identified strong correlations with finances and other behaviors in accordance with this 20-year study. I met with people for no less than one hour, from the east coast to the west coast and in between to develop a substantial understanding of commitments and marriage, and what constitutes success.

Intelligence isn't always the greatest indication of ability to make decisions that are triumphant. I have a very intelligent friend who is a celebrated professor at a highly regarded Los Angeles University. As he walked down the aisle to be married, his intuition desperately tried to stop him like disruptive thunder. Unfortunately, he regrets that he ignored this sign. He became one of the most miserable and tortured divorcees I have ever seen. I highly doubt this very "book smart" man will doubt his intuition again. Even the blessing, which is his daughter, is an object to be fought over. There are an infinite number of stories such as this one. Many people justify marrying a person that the gut warns us to avoid. By fully comprehending his experience, we can all choose to avoid turmoil in the future. We all must seriously follow the signs. Signs are everywhere. Most people are so busy sleepwalking, listening to music, watching TV, and playing with their smart phones that they wouldn't recognize a sign if it hit them in the head.

Some people have a hard time deciding what they want for lunch. Deciding what you want for lunch is not a difficult decision; you know what you are not supposed to eat, whether you will admit it or not. Big decisions usually require mindfulness and silence for contemplation. It is always amazing to see how much wisdom materializes when we give that wisdom a chance to appear.

If you have no experience whatsoever with your still, small voice, you must awaken it. For me, ideas and answers appear like billboards; they flash in my mind at any given time. I know, with some practice you can also enjoy such revelations.

For me, this still, small voice will usually come as an idea. When I quietly consult with that wisdom which is within me, guiding me, the answer I receive is rarely a simple "yes" or "no". You may find that your intuition gives you straightforward answers at times. My intuition also often screams at me before I have a chance to mindfully contemplate the issue. This is a major timesaver, especially when I need to say no and can move on to the next thing on my agenda. Getting clearer has always been and will always be a major challenge for humans. Although I often enjoy the gift of intuition, once in a while I am dumbfounded. It may take several times of contemplation to reap the answer I seek.

Getting connected to your inner self is the beginning and also most challenging. It will allow our judgmental and critical observations to be eclipsed by something bigger and more powerful, *and* it is always right. I hope you are ready to hear what is waiting to come out. The challenge in this exercise is to know the difference between your inner wisdom and your ego; this is learned over time. For most, including myself, intuition is the voice of God and a Universal Intelligence that is far larger than my life's intelligence. It filters through my purpose and I can express it in my own unique way.

> *"When the solution is simple, God is answering."*
>
> ~ Albert Einstein

(I guess Einstein agrees with me.)

This chapter may seem the most difficult step of the seven, and it may take practice. The good news is that it can simultaneously work to improve your health and longevity. It can also improve *all* of your relationships. It is not uncommon for people to have little or no confidence in their intuitive abilities. Most people try to deny this gut instinct and will instead listen to their negative subconscious thoughts and fears. This is tragic. Recognizing and categorizing your internal voices will help you distinguish the validity of these messages. Discernment comes with practice. It is often the case that those who try meditation may quit before they begin to receive the messages they seek. Sometimes the intuition won't give its human the instant gratification that he or she is seeking and the subconscious mind is quick to give negative answers, which are usually wrong.

Many New Age ideas seem ridiculous to intelligent people. Meditation isn't really New Age. What most don't understand is that this practice has been performed for thousands of years; there is nothing new about meditation.

Psychics have happily been receiving messages for profit for their clients and it may seem easier to employ a more 'spiritual' person to do the work. There are Mystics and there are Psychics. In all fairness, all Psychics are not wrong. When you don't accept the challenge to look inside yourself, you will be denied many breakthroughs as well as clear instruction that you may appreciate. Answers and revelations are best received by the one seeking the revelation. It is also possible that discipline and focus is difficult to achieve for certain people. It is simply a matter of learning to relax for those who are impatient. Finally, as difficult as it may seem to start this practice, I promise you that your wrong decisions will cause more difficulty in your life than taking some time to relax physically. Resting and rejuvenating emotionally and mentally will allow greater productivity as well as greater decision-making. Meditation alone will assist you to achieve an overall improvement, benefiting your whole life. Trying to talk yourself out of utilizing meditation in your life at this point would be absolutely self-destructive, not to mention eccentric and unconventional.

There are many ways to receive your messages. You may see them with your eyes open or closed, as I do. You may hear the message when no sound is perceptible around you. Stranger things have happened; you may meet your message in the form of a sign or a human being. It is also possible that your other senses, such as taste, smell, or feel may reveal your message. Because I am a deeply spiritual person, at times I will ask God to show me a sign. I almost always easily recognize that which I am seeking. When you decide to look for a sign, simply ask that it is something that is easily understood by you, within plain sight; this is how I ask.

No matter who you are, no matter where you have been, or what you have gone through, you are the source of your own wisdom. Because we have all made mistakes, this can be hard to swallow. There is no lack or limitation within you. *All limitations are imagined. I cannot be more serious about this.* If this is the only thing you take from this book, you will be richer in every aspect of your life. Even if this makes no sense to you right now, give this theory a try. Give meditation a try and prove this to yourself as quickly as possible, of course, without applying any pressure to yourself. Relax, and know that you are no different than anyone else. We are all spiritual beings. It is not possible that one being is more spiritual than another. In human life, we are all spiritual beings having a human experience, as I mentioned already in other words. Spiritual beings do not suffer, but in the human form we experience pain. As you recognize yourself as a spiritual being, you will not suffer as much. I have been telling patients for quite some time, "Suffering is optional." You can learn to turn off suffering like you can turn off your television by reframing an event. You are always in total control of yourself. *Understand that your choices up until now have formed your life, creating positive or negative experiences. Your life is and will always be a product of your decisions.* Do you see the magnitude of decision-making? As humans, we are all challenged in ways and at times that boggle the mind. No one said life would be easy. Meditation makes life easier. Knowing what to do will turn difficulties into simple situations. If the whole world would meditate and discern the valuable messages within each and every person, we would have a very productive, unbelievably wealthy, absolutely helpful and compassionate world to enjoy. Some of us will learn to read the messages that are within us. Can you afford not to dedicate time and effort to the practice of meditation? I think not. More importantly, *what do you think?* Obviously, this is a good time to think.

It matters not if you choose to consider meditation a religious practice. It is true that the prophets of all religions have utilized meditation, and many have urged others to do the same. At the same time, I will reiterate that meditation is not really a religious practice at all. *Are you feeling resistance to meditation?* You may not want to invest the time or rest the mind, but it pays back dividends.

If you were considering skipping this step, the blessing of intuition, I hope you have settled on shaving off 15 to 30 minutes here and there to pay homage to the wisdom within yourself. Now, let's transform your life, if this is new for you.

The first lesson of using your intuition is to listen to the still, small voice within you. In a world of constant commotion, music, noise, smart phones, TV, car radios, infinite static, and other interruptions, we have a challenge in finding spiritual connection. Stillness is not something given, it is something taken. Steal the time you need, but schedule it the best you can. In order to find a serene, quiet place to get in touch with your inner wisdom, you will have to take responsibility for proactively facilitating it. In order to see the answers within yourself, you will establish a quiet place without disturbances and interruptions. This may be in your home. This place may be in nature. You will need to turn off your phone and be certain that no one will bother you when you are taking this time to look inside yourself.

In a completely calm place, you will be able to discover who you really are. Your blueprint will come alive in living color as you recognize your purpose and all that you must do in this life. Decision-making will become immeasurably easier than it has ever been before. Many breakthroughs are available to those who can sit in the stillness and turn within to see the answers that are inside.

At this point, recognize that looking all around and asking others' opinions, as well as following general consensus is of little benefit to you. You may necessarily choose to do research before making a decision. However, keep this research factual rather than asking the opinions of others. Your sources need to be reliable. Your intuition will certainly facilitate that others will be pleased with your decision if they care for you. Satisfaction all around you will be granted. When I make a decision, I try to express my Creator and please myself, and naturally, if God is pleased, others will be pleased. Many people will tell you this, however, much of this idea is misused and manipulates other people. When you are asked to subscribe to opinions that are hurtful or manipulative, you are not following a spiritual path. Learning to use the intuition suggests that we can wear blinders. Just as a carriage driver puts blinders on the horses, we will want to advance based on inner revelation rather than the surrounding traffic, ego and ideas that are 'band aids' instead of true solutions.

Meditation is the most effective form in which to seek inner revelation. There are a growing number of people who are not religious but claim to be spiritual while using meditation to align themselves with the God of their understanding. Consider that there is something valuable in every religion that can shed light in a darkness. In fact, if you are to attend a place of worship, only your own inner self can lead you to that religion. Any thinking person would happily adopt spiritual practices, recognizing that they are at one with other beings and nature. Knowing this oneness exists is a very powerful force in making decisions, as well as its impact on everyday living. Again, disrespecting others will not bring anyone to the outcome they seek. If it is not abundantly clear, breakthroughs, revelations, and practices suggested by this book in no way denounces any religion. Anyone can use this information to make better decisions. When we choose to come from a higher place, rather than a place of emotional swings, sleepwalking or automatic pilot, better decisions are absolutely the result. Directing your own mind is powerful.

Developing a higher consciousness is key in making all of the decisions in your life. Free yourself from tension and anger, and you will be able to see what is truly important. When we are angry, we seek change or to do damage. Anger may be a sign for a need to change, but remember, decisions are better made from a place of contentment and peace. I always say *what angers you, conquers you*. In aligning yourself with serenity and silence rather than stress and agitation, you will facilitate brilliant decisions.

Meditation can be helpful in as little as 15 minutes, and often, with practice, any time spent is valuable. Consider "power naps". In times when an immediate decision is necessary, you may not be able to do more than take a few deep breaths to calm yourself. It is highly preferable to calmly breathe before making a decision of importance rather than reacting fearfully. Reacting is not a very evolved process. Proactive creating is far more desirable and more powerful. Notice how many times you may have reacted when you were angry. Often an uncomfortable situation escalates and the comfort you seek is pushed farther from your reach. Reacting never seems to stabilize the situation, it normally makes circumstances worse. Learning to make decisions using inner wisdom rather than reacting may be the single most important intelligent practice learned by many people. There is a much-underestimated anger problem in the world today. It would be wise for anyone to become part of the solution rather than increasing our very obvious collective anger issue. Impatience and frustration are merely the consequences of anger and tend to slow the process of resolution, rather than quickening it. When all people recognize that wise and deliberate action creates a positive change faster than demanding that others hurry up, we will all live in .a more productive and satisfying world.

There are certainly times we must take immediate action. Later, I promise to address this situation in which you must act without time to employ this 7-Step decision-making process. For now, let's introduce mindful meditation.

At times, we don't achieve clarity, or nothing will come to us. If you must make a decision without your intuition's input, move forward and proceed with your best answer logically. The most important thing that you may gain from this chapter is to recognize your intuition and follow signs, regardless of whether you have ever paid any mind to intuition before. This is a tough lesson for many. In the future, when you see trouble, just walk away. Heed the warnings of your gut. Yes, this is a matter of learning to trust yourself, but it really rewards those with this mindful patience. The voice within you is looking out for your highest good. You can rely upon it.

Let's not address lofty goals such as enlightenment now. That is a byproduct. By making great decisions in a consistent manner, you will earn your Ph.D. in life. You can *doctor yourself* with spiritual practice that improves your entire life. You need not reinvent the wheel to feel powerful and enjoy your mind and spirit.

You may be challenged by the origin of the messages you begin to receive. We can learn and discern our conscious thoughts from our subconscious, the ego, the emotions, and race consciousness. Collective thoughts of humans, such as societal beliefs and prejudices characterize race consciousness. We all must supersede this way of thinking, even if we believe we are not bigots. Your advancement will not be a struggle. You will simply learn to see through thoughts that are interim social agreements, not necessarily formed by yourself. We can learn to see through concepts that we have heard multiple times from others. In modern America, advertising and marketing fills our lives with 'needs' that are not important at all. I find true power in deciding what I really want to buy instead of what advertising agencies are trying to manipulate me to accept as my own need or belief. With this in mind, I enjoy spending money all the more. I can also enjoy spending less.

Your conscious mind may express your desires more genuinely than your subconscious mind. Unfortunately, it is the subconscious mind that will dictate all of your actions. You may be interested to know that your subconscious mind is responsible for any underachieving you have agreed to accept. The subconscious mind delights in taking shortcuts, quitting, and keeping life simple in an unproductive way for the majority of people. It can be common to see hard-working people sell themselves short because the subconscious mind is concerned with seeking comfort. The subconscious mind and the ego can team up and deny many desires of the conscious mind. It is uncommon for people to walk their talk because of this sucking force that believes in limitation, lack, and an unproductive means of self- preservation. The greatest pain of my life has come at times I have chosen not to persevere and not to achieve. If this pain resonates with you, now is the time to recognize it and become bigger than it. It won't be easy, it might even be lonely at the top, but self-actualization is worth the exertion. The ego will certainly try to convince you that you do not want to be lonely at the top; the deceiving message says it will be too hard and that comfort is in the status quo. When we resist the ego, eventually the exertion overcomes, just like adrenaline turns to bliss with physical exercise. The resistance lessens until it is gone, and smooth sailing follows. It is a beautiful thing. I hope you go for it.

The intuitive mind may also rear its head. At times, we think we *just know*. It feels real.

Recognizing any emotional thoughts or behavior can be easy. When you suspect that your emotions are trying to direct you, examine the real sadness, anger, or other emotion and its true origin *from the past*. Emotions are histrionic, melodramatic and exaggerating theatrics. The subconscious mind, race consciousness, the ego, and the emotions are all rooted in the past. If your conscious mind wants a truly loving relationship or to achieve something wonderful, don't allow the past to interfere. The past acts as a horrendous dream stealer - don't allow it.

Joy and elation are different. These emotions are truly wonderful and powerful. These extraordinary feelings are a book all by themselves. Love can fit into this mold, but first we must learn if we are experiencing love or infatuation. *Are we experiencing love or attachment?* Love is the highest and most powerful emotion, but sadly, love gets a bad rap too often, because it is used to disguise lesser situations and emotions. The desire to avoid being alone is far from love; this is a call for therapy and a warning not to engage in romance at that time.

Differentiating can be learned by anyone. Commit to self-examination for awhile and decision-making will become easier in a short time. Humans can really make life difficult by doing everything on autopilot. Truly, most people choose not to think. They aren't really even making decisions; they are simply reacting and accepting whatever comes, happily or miserably. We are now learning to think so that we can advance into a life of more pleasures and less challenges. Keep that in mind and success will be your result.

Meditation will allow you to seek the truth within you, as you enjoy momentous health benefits. Your brain is made up of white and gray matter. The gray matter includes cell bodies, axons, and dendrites, so your brain can increase its number of neurons with meditation. This is great news in a world where so many people worry about losing their brain cells. Meditators report a much greater level of everyday happiness than those who do not meditate.

Often, it doesn't feel like it, but you are allowed to discover, be free, and escape stress. You will have your moments at home, at work, or somewhere in chaos when you need this tranquility, even thousands of miles from here, and you will have that peace. You can learn to find the eye of the storm— it is a peaceful place for contemplation. You can overcome the storm.

Meditation is stripping the mind to its foundation in search of certainty. Logic tells us our awareness may have another side. We will seek that which is behind our awareness. To reach the highest goal, the discovery of one's true nature, this requires scientific logic and intuition, which is the still, small voice within you.

People everywhere attribute better health, better relationships, clarity, peace, and a greater ability to earn money, to meditation. We can enjoy these benefits through Western meditation, which can be characterized as a mindful or a concentrated state of mind in serious reflection.

The Latin root of the word meditation, *mederi* means "to heal." Meditation heals afflictions of the mind and a hurt ego. It facilitates understanding the cause of a 'problem' and finding the solution, deepening a state of understanding.

Too much mental exercise can lead to tension and confusion. According to Zen, meditation does not involve any concept, but is an awareness of inner silence. This is often known as Mindful Meditation.

In some forms of meditation, you may adopt a Mantra. This is often known as Concentration Meditation. In Sanskrit, *mantra* literally means 'a tool of thought.' For me, an affirmation is a mantra. Mantras are said to cleanse and enlighten the mind, however there is no real evidence. I am certain a mantra can heal insecurities rooted in the subconscious mind. From a standpoint of making decisions, I would advise mindful meditation, without mantras. Affirmations can also be spoken aloud (any time of the day) if you would like to program a tool of thought or a mindset. Affirmations are a very powerful tool to overcome weaknesses that may limit you. Affirmations are typically done in a conscious state.

If you would like help creating a powerful and appropriate custom affirmation for yourself, visit a web page I posted for my patients: www.bestdecisionforyou.com/affirmations.

Yes, affirmations are for everyone and they work across the board. Everyone benefits from affirmations, so I recommend doing them every day.

Now is the time to stop struggling and to surrender to the good that is within your being. This may be an important method of discerning your good from the incessant chatter that battles against everything you want in life. It is possible that waiting for a delicate, still, small voice may cause you to shake or quake. Such religions as Shakers and Quakers have experienced these effects. Don't try to institute physical activity and don't try to fight it either. It is very likely that you will have an extremely relaxing experience that will rejuvenate you and bring energy to you after this short time, as a bonus. Remember, you are always safe in meditation.

> *"I think 99 times and find nothing. I stop thinking, swim in silence, and the truth comes to me."*
>
> ~ Albert Einstein

The Benefits of Intuition

If you can really learn to listen for your intuition and use it, this alone may be your most powerful tool for making decisions. You will also feel happy about implementing those decisions because you are following your heart or gut.

Psychologically speaking, we can use affirmations and mantras, while conscious or in a trance, to reprogram the subconscious mind. You can experience spiritual renewal, the feeling of oneness with a higher source of life (God, the spiritual truth, the Universe, etc.) and find a deep state of peace. As you search for basic truths in life, you will separate your reality from illusion. You will acquire a clear understanding of your desired reality rather than confusing it with a foggy, thoughtless state. With practice, one can develop philosophical maturity and acquire purity of heart, freedom from resentment, hate, prejudice, and negative thinking.

The Implementation

Now, if you can do these steps, you can meditate...

First, control your ENVIRONMENT. Make sure all is quiet, with or without soft music ---no phones, radio, or TV.

Next, attend to your SITTING and posture. Sit comfortably in a chair or on the floor (or cushion), positioning your neck, shoulders, and back straight. Remain alert with adequate breathing. Your legs may be crossed or uncrossed. Lotus (which is sort of a 'leg pretzel') or 1/2 lotus position looks impressive but is unnecessary.

Now you might take a second or two to notice your BREATHING. Your breathing will find its own rhythm. Breathe a rich supply of oxygen if possible.

Better oxygen=Better breathing

Your cadence will regulate itself to a perfect speed. Breathing characterizes:

- *Retention-it raises the body' s temperature and oxygen is absorbed*

- *Exhalation-toxic air is released into the atmosphere*

- *Inhalation-it stimulates the whole body and gives life*

    Don't hold your breath. You will naturally pick a style of circulating air comfortably. There is a technique known as

"Belly Breathing" that you may choose to employ. Yogis believe these concepts: Belly breathing energizes mental processes. The force that animates all matter is prana, as "pranayama" studies this. Belly breathing produces higher levels of prana, thus a clearer consciousness. Focus on the inflowing prana deep inside the head and nerve cells.

Mindful Meditation

Beginners: Close your eyes. *Focus on your breath and dismiss all other thoughts. Consider OBSERVING as even focus requires active thought versus passive observation.*

This is the last step to mention before you actually meditate: You may bring the question to the forefront of your mind before you begin, but then clear your mind until it's empty. As you settle, dismiss all thoughts. If this is a challenge, count your breaths and focus on breathing to relieve these distractions. Your mind may wander and think about pressing issues that are unrelated, or it may begin to justify some sort of decision. KEEP YOUR MIND CLEAR and literally look for an empty place in your mind. When the answer you seek comes, you will know, but don't expect it while you are in mediation. Spend 15-30 minutes in silence. You will improve with practice.

The Cost of Ignoring Your Intuition

You will justify decisions instead, which feels good for a moment; it's a smug satisfaction. You will feel validated but not solve the issue; it leaves an empty feeling to follow. Wrong decisions are costly in every way.

Decide to have faith in your plans, yourself, and your intuition.

This is a difficult concept for so many people. Your Universal Truth is...*It is done unto you as you believe.* This is why you must see yourself in a positive light. You gain when you have the faith to succeed---to move forward expecting the best. If you do not expect to finish, you will not take the steps necessary. Often things turn out better than we can imagine when we move ahead on the course and expect fully to finish victoriously. I do it. My personal lesson #1 was not to quit. I mastered it. If you have problems with faith, grasp onto that concept and always live by moving forward. You can even fail forward, and the most likely thing that happens is we can see something even better within reach. Maybe you are on the course toward something that isn't viable. If you proceed with faith, you will see your destination, and you will land in a wonderful place at the end of the journey. I remember that I was driven to pursue a career in front of the cameras in Hollywood. I moved to L.A., acquired an agent and started going to auditions, studying, and getting some work. I had some recurring parts on General Hospital as well as many prime-time TV shows. I had small parts in big films and big parts in small films. As I learned that stardom wouldn't't really make me happy, this hunger caused me to find ways to improve myself as well as others. This personal development kick turned out well for me. I was given a TV show about physical fitness also illustrating how the principles that worked in the gym work in every aspect of daily life. I was the creator of this show, which people were often unaware. We began in just 3 markets— New York, Chicago, and L.A. As this spirited show evolved, eventually we were self-syndicating into 186 cities or markets, as we say in the television business. The infamous Joe Weider gave his endorsement on air. He said, "People couldn't get better information, no matter where they looked." Weider published *Shape, Muscle and Fitness* and other huge selling magazines. Jack LaLanne was a guest twice. Major TV stars and Academy Award winning actors were guests as well. This show ran about 4 years, which in the television industry, is a very good run. It was viewed usually on UPN, FOX, and NBC stations throughout the U.S. I got fan mail that warmed my heart, and occasionally my eyes teared in joy. My mission was defined. I saw what I was meant to be, and it helped others. I was gracious and not afraid to laugh at myself. Life rewarded me for my efforts and all that I had learned. I promise you, life is like that. If this was failure, *I'll take some more failure, please.*

Choose to be open-minded instead of closed-minded.

In order to do this, one must be open-minded enough to know what *open-minded is.*

> *"Mediocre minds usually dismiss anything which reaches beyond their own understanding."*
>
> ~ Francois, Duc del la Rochefoucauld

I came from the Midwest and in my experience, it is almost impossible to avoid accepted opinions. People form judgments and cannot see outside of those beliefs to save their lives. I value the steadfastness (also known to be stubbornness) that I learned in Chicagoland, however, I would be far less successful in every way (by settling for less and believing in less) if I had not lived most of my adult life in the land of open-mindedness: Southern California. I do not suggest being gullible. Listening and using logic is important if you want to succeed. Being open requires wearing an imaginary thinking cap; keep discerning truth so that you don't get swept out to sea.

Albert Einstein said, *"The only thing that interferes with my learning is my education."* This is the obstacle that I had to overcome, and it pays dividends. Remember, we need to be ready for change in this day and age.

> *"People only see what they are prepared to see."*
>
> ~ Ralph Waldo Emerson

**STEP #7
Empowerment is Your
Path**

Most of us don't feel empowered or operate under this positive force for progress. The vast population sleepwalks on autopilot through their days. We don't see others operate under this conscious and joyous feeling often enough. Empowerment takes the high road while its polar opposite of 'making decisions to avoid pain' travels the low road. Quite simply, avoiding pain constitutes the criteria for most decisions that the average person makes. Rather than fear, doubt, and worry as a guide, we move forward exhilarated. We feel aligned with everything and everyone when we are empowered. It is a tremendous feeling in which you lose track of time as you create something that excites you. We are all empowered by different outcomes. Some people want to help the poor, and still others want to build widgets, and this makes them happy. As long as we are helping somebody and not damaging others, the planet, or ourselves we will feel empowered to develop a worthy mission in the realm of subject matter that personally excites us.

When people are empowered, they make good decisions. Generally, what do people *want* out of life?

- To love and be loved

- Family and belonging

- Recognition

- Self-esteem

- Self-actualization

- Immediate income to live

- Residual income to work when we need rest

- A sound plan for the future

- Unexpected and expected bonuses and happy surprises

- To own their own business, earn more money, or to be the boss

- To have fun at work and outside work

- To feel aligned with one's beliefs, and in integrity

- To feel content and complete instead of frustrated

- To be physically healthy instead of bodily impaired

Empowered people attain all or many of these objectives. This is due to the positive nature of their minds and bodies at work. Feeling great and emitting this energy attracts positive people and desirable opportunities into one's life. Empowered people are usually also proactive versus reactive when they attend to their various business. When you are excited and psyched up, you will be a self-starter who makes things happen and creates positive change. Reactive people are usually the sleepwalkers that excessively watch TV and wait to be chased or prodded. On the other hand, proactive people can become so busy that a few things slip through the cracks, so don't assume people are always sleepwalkers just because you aren't seeing progress.

For as long as humankind has been in existence, we have taken manifestation and physical form to fulfill a purpose. Productive people agree with this, therefore, in order to embody the sexy and purposeful life of 'the powerful' that is highly desirable to some, please decide to accept this as another un-evidenced theory that will fall into place and make perfect sense later. As it becomes your reality, it will be totally natural, empowering, and suitable. Your potential is divinity in its essence, and the Divine takes human form to fulfill a purpose. Those who discover their individual purpose feel that expressing it takes them into a place where time does not matter because fulfilling this purpose ignites joy. Naming it simply 'flow,' psychologist, Mihaly Csikszentmihályi became fascinated by artists who would essentially get "lost" in their work, and he is said to have coined the term "flow" to describe what Deepak Chopra describes as "timeless awareness."

Are you motivated to do something??? Maybe so, but if not, you have not yet figured out your life's passion or purpose. When I am doing something that I feel has purpose, I can hardly stop myself from working. This aids your chances to finish without quitting and makes it uplifting as well.

There is something within you, waiting to be done. It is your life's purpose and you do indeed have passion for it. Most people don't know what their purpose is. Many people are clouded by their ego. There is a tragic trend right now. People want to be famous. *Famous for what?* Too many don't care by what means, which I would argue could include murder, fighting in a subway, or other unproductive behavior. This is how shows like Jerry Springer stay on the air; people want to air their dirty laundry and to be on TV. They also want to be validated or vindicated and we will address that later, too. If you can get the ego out of the way, there is something you can do that helps others that will *really* make you want to jump out of bed every morning. Let's try to identify your purpose. Everyone has a purpose in life. Trust me regarding this matter, and you will find yours and articulate it. In return, I will believe in you.

Are you typically bored? People without purpose tend to need to be entertained, but don't worry, there is an exciting, purpose-filled life for everyone. Perhaps you have a blueprint inside you that you have not read yet. To make great decisions, you need to know who you really are. I designed this process, so you could make the perfect decision for you but first, you need to know who you are. I can tell you, you are a divine being, unfolding and developing to your highest potential. Discover your purpose. I made a transformational tool called "Reinvent Yourself *Earn Big Money without Competition by Doing What You Love*." Listen to the audio exercises and let your paper and pen tell you what will make you jump out of bed, excited, ready for that flow to take you on a great adventure, and yes, this journey creates monetary compensation. You may even want to reinvent yourself many times through life.

Your # 1 decision at hand may have little to do with your purpose, but when you are discovering and fulfilling your purpose, you will find that all decisions become easier because so much of what is available to consider will not be worth the effort, and you have more time to do what matters most to you.

If your decision seems unrelated to work, please bear with this step so you can make better decisions now and in the future. You may quickly discover some of your past decision-making flaws.

It has been said, "God doesn't make junk," therefore we know everyone has a purpose. For now, just give this theory the benefit of the doubt. It will serve you if you allow it. Please accept that everyone possesses a unique gift or special talent to share with others. When we blend this unique talent with service to others, we experience joy and exultation within ourselves. This is the ultimate goal of all goals in life. This is characterized by <u>Maslow's Hierarchy of Needs</u>, showing self-actualization on the top of the pyramid. With this purpose, also known as Dharma, we experience love during work, producing more self-love continuously. Dharma is a Sanskrit word that means purpose in life and essentially refers to Cosmic Law, and in the Buddha's teaching refers to the moral life of all beings in relation to that Law. Buddha gave the Dharma in the Four Noble Truths, and the Noble Eightfold Path, and in effect it is the teaching of how to live a compassionate and conscious life.

When challenged, as something pulls you up to meet the goal in a stronger manner than gravity pulls you down, that is the "Infinite Power" within that fortifies and furnishes strength beyond what the mind and body believe is possible. This is how I describe the use of body, mind, and spirit together that allows us to become so immersed in our intention that we can exceed our abilities and known potential.

In addition, because we are all so incredibly unique, we can specialize in specific niches that will create greater enjoyment for us while working and increase the appreciation that customers, subscribers, or users will give to enjoy this work.

Each person has a unique talent and a unique way of expressing it. There is something that each individual on Earth can do better than anyone else in the whole world. For every unique talent and unique expression of that talent, there are also unique needs. When these needs are matched with the creative expression of your talents - that is the spark that creates affluence. In expressing your talents to fulfill needs, wealth and abundance is created.

One of the reasons that individuals suffer in their workplaces is that this work may impair the act of discovering his or her true self. (I will address this with a feasible plan in coming pages.) This is something in the essence of any given person. Any person will at times experience this essence, spirit, or soul within themselves, wishing to express a purpose. This is true in all people, regardless of their religious beliefs. The thought may not resonate well with every individual, but we are not human beings that have occasional spiritual experiences, it's the other way around—we're spiritual beings that have occasional human experiences. These human experiences are the source of pain in our lives. Those who have adopted spiritual beliefs know that they are spiritual beings that have taken manifestation in physical form. Their souls wish to express something unique, useful, and divine. This is where purpose fits into his or her life.

After we have found the purpose that is trying to express through our actions and work, and we have used the unique talent that is expressed individually, service to humanity will cause the success that perpetuates this entire equation. Instead of asking the question, "What's in it for me?" the dialogue is better shifted to, "How can I help?" When one thinks and works for gratification beyond the ego, all things are made possible. "How am I best suited to serve humanity?" is the question, and putting this into practice is the answer. All in all, matching the needs of fellow human beings with the desire to help and serve others will allow your purpose to be successful.

As you begin to dabble in what brings you great joy and purpose, feel free to hold onto your job or source of income. You can phase it out in time, but don't give up what you feel the need to express. Your purpose is a major factor in your decisions. Don't be sidetracked by going in an opposing direction because it seems like a good idea at the time. Those who stay home, waiting for opportunities to express their purpose often find that they have failed to meet their needs, and that becomes so uncomfortable that it is increasingly difficult to express their passion or purpose. You are more likely to find the perfect outlet for your purpose by working a job that is not your purpose than by staying home and hoping for the perfect opportunity. It may not seem so, but your efforts and energy will find the correct place for you faster when you are already exerting energy and showing up with a song in your heart.

Maybe you are not clear on your purpose or a passion so great you could see yourself in the state of flow; don't worry. Ask yourself, if money was of no concern and you had sufficient free time, what would you do? If you have a passion for what you do, that passion creates the joy and feeling of purpose. You can find a niche in which to work that will eventually serve the needs of others. When humanity is serviced well, money follows, even if it is not immediate. Some people who do good work in the service of others will tell you this simply isn't so because their pessimism won't allow them to carry on long enough to evidence the fruits of their labor. You must persist and experience the joy. The path will become clear to you if you listen to your inner voice rather than justification and ego.

EMPOWERMENT=PASSION=PURPOSE

There is a relationship between your purpose, the work that is generated as you express this purpose and making money in this process. The principle of earning money from the work that is valued by others is an exchange of energy. Economics express this exchange of appreciated work for money. This is also a metaphysical principle, proven to be true in this Universe through physics and quantum physics. For those who are not well-versed in the connections between consciousness and the material world, it will become obvious how it equates to monetary return. What you give is what you get, metaphysically speaking, and if you collect money for services instead of refusing payment or bartering, money can be received and continue to accumulate as the good or service continues to be appreciated. It is also true that others have become wealthy by using the barter system. We will not discount any methods of payment for now. These are only details. The next section will address this relationship and illustrate the divine consequence of receiving a monetary return for your work. This is important because many people have adverse relationships with money that cause them to underachieve, just to spite money. Money, in and of itself, is not evil. The fear of being successful will inhibit the benefits and self-actualization that one derives from working freely with their purpose. Making a difference in the lives of others will increase self-esteem by doing so, but fear of making money will interfere with this whole divine process. The sections to follow will direct these concerns.

Many decisions that people make are dependent on money. I do not suggest that people live beyond their financial means, and if you are not able to save 10% of your income, I call that living above your means.

In order to do more of what you love and use your time on things you enjoy, you will need money. Many of my decisions include travel. I lecture on six continents and enjoy seeing the world. My decisions often include venturing to new places or doing add-on trips when I am done working. I need money to do this. I want you to make decisions based on your interests rather than having to decline due to a lack of funds. If others have earned and saved more than they have required, this is also possible for you. It is a spiritual principle.

Decide to wake up; awareness is the key to all opportunity.

Awareness is one of the most helpful attributes you can develop. In making our decisions, we find more options when our field of view expands. Just the thought of living without sight, hearing, or touch is devastating, but having them is almost as sure as taking them for granted. Awareness is the key to finding opportunity and meeting the people we want to encounter.

If we could have complete omniscience, we could avoid all accidents, travel trouble-free, and find anything or anyone. This is a great reason to become aware; it begins to bridge gaps. We will deal better and more efficiently with others with every extra detail we can learn, preventing offensiveness and misunderstandings. We seize more known opportunities and experience less missed opportunities. If we had total cognition, knowing things as fact instead of opinion or belief, we could perform perfectly. Many people accept their beliefs as absolute fact. *Are you still one of them?* This behavior will surely add frustration to anyone's life.

Personally, when I realized the power in awareness, I could find more opportunities and do more to help others. That increased my actual productivity. By knowing what the World needs, you can give them what they are requesting. There is no profit in placating your ego; just do what is needed.

Knowing what upsets others will allow us to keep them calm by avoiding these behaviors. We can also decide we don't wish to deal with such people. When we know what others enjoy, we can complement their experiences with what they like. Trying to sell to someone without first asking what they want, and what criteria are essential, is a waste of breath. It's not likely someone will buy something they don't want in the first place.

We benefit by doing everything we can to obtain the greatest awareness possible. This would not include invading the privacy of others or breaking the law. If you feel this is necessary for your quest, you are creating a very negative situation. If you stub your toe, you will experience pain, and most likely anger. Exercising care seems like a great idea after these incidents occur. Aside from that, consider the possibility that any person may have self-destructive tendencies. If you are aware of these tendencies, protect yourself and others. Awareness can prevent injury as well as mental and physical pain. Added awareness increases pleasure and decreases suffering.

In the acquisition of money, finding opportunity and knowing what the masses want to buy is essential. There is a similarity in meeting the love of your life and enrolling them into a relationship. Keep your eyes and ears open and resist the urge to do all the talking. You could be missing the doors that must be passed through, causing the end result to fail by not going through proper channels.

While you develop greater awareness, the other distinctions in this chapter will serve you well. Sometimes you may not have the time to get the news, the e-mails, and check with your sources, but these concepts will serve you in all situations.

Decide to be rich without guilt.

Most people are misdirected into believing "money is the power" as opposed to the earning potential held by every living individual. Basically, the role of currency isn't 'King.' Once we are open to taking money out of the highest position, placing ourselves there instead, we can begin to understand where the power to manifest wealth lies. Let's see this as it applies to the United States and other democratic countries.

We, the people, gave currency its value. We created it. We probably spend more time trying to accumulate money than improving our own minds, bodies, and spirits.

Currency itself does not farm food, design and assemble a car, or create the infrastructure of a city. We can claim power in our own artistic gifts and feel comfortable knowing this.

Long ago there was no currency. People simply bartered for their wants and needs. If we could get all that was available without dealing in currency, and simply with what products and services we produced and practiced, that would be proof that money isn't worth more than the paper it's printed on. We know, therefore, that currency isn't actually necessary. It was a convenience that has unfortunately become worshipped by many who forgot that at one time, the world survived without almighty dollars.

Money is only money. After talent, skills, or power is developed by anyone, that individual can acquire as much currency as they are not afraid to earn.

People aren't your source and supply. A company isn't your source of income. It is every individual's inherent talent, effort, or gift that brings forth funds. If money is a challenge for you, take the power away from monetary notes, and put the power back into yourself.

Decide to think positive, set intentions, and 'will' your outcome.

You must know what you want, and be definite about it. Vague desires are no foundation for success. If you're not sure about what you want to create, spend as much leisure time as you can contemplating this picture. Get the image and fix it in your mind as an imperative goal. Also know that things will change in your life drastically to handle all of this success. Welcome this change or forget the dream.

Your desire to be successful must be strong enough to hold you to this vision or purpose. You must be strong enough to overcome a life of laziness.

> *"One person with a belief is equal to a force of ninety-nine who have only interest."*
>
> ~ John Stuart Mill

You must take possession of this vision in your mind, knowing that it is already yours. When you feel at one with it, you can proceed to get the work done to experience it all in material form.

Obviously, doing nothing is not a way to take delivery of such manifestations. This starts with a sort of visioning process. Anyone can have a vision, big or small. *I know this sounds difficult, but how else could people become self-made millionaires and billionaires?* I can assure you, they weren't thinking small. There was no accident and the intentions they had were held and believed 24 hours a day. The thought of quitting sets in when we don't believe. Quitters never win, and winners never quit. In fact, you haven't failed until you have given up. Failures can become millionaires, but quitters cannot. We may fail several times before succeeding. Patience may be necessary. Exercise patience to the extreme if necessary. Put blinders on, but don't stop until you reach the goal.

This is how you can experience the perfect mate, a fit body, or anything you wish to experience. It does not govern over finances only. We can create anything.

I cannot stress the importance of believing that your vision is real and done. Don't tell people that you own a ten-million-dollar mansion and drive a Rolls Royce if it's not true, but picture yourself every day at the house and driving the car. If you prefer to run a big foundation that helps a group of people, picture that. Tailor your visioning process. Don't lie but focus on the vision and it will manifest eventually. If you know that succeeding with your purpose will create wealth, picture yourself going to work, walking through the physical location, or on the Internet or phone in a luxurious setting. You must believe this is a done deal, or you will settle for other concepts and ideas that will become obstacles, and you will never arrive at the vision. Climbing the ladder is quite different than settling. I am a big proponent of gaining experience and becoming an expert; this is powerful. Often the actual outcome exceeds the picture we imagined. This is one of the wonders of the plan and what holds it sacred. Faith, purpose, and imagination can discern between the dreamer and 'the scientist.' Since this is proven to work for people of all kinds, it is key to stay with the science and arrive at the vision instead of thinking about it. This has been a successful formula for myself and also hundreds of people I have interviewed. Focus, stay the course and don't worry that you won't make it.

The other most important thing to keep in the forefront of your mind is your intention. Thinking about your intention is quite different than thinking about what could go wrong, even in trying to prevent these disasters. Complete every task with dotted i's and crossed t's and your troubles will be few. Never frustrate yourself with potential problems. Just do the work the best it can be done. Everyone has challenges, but why bring yourself down while you're rising to the vision you desire to create? Negative thoughts of complications will only take the wind out of your sails. Feel free to be prepared and have back up plans for glitches; these allow us to step out without worry. My point is that no one ever got rich contemplating or studying poverty. All of the consideration and knowledge of poverty has not rid any place of it. This does not recommend hard-heartedness. You can hear and answer the cry of need without actually investigating it. In fact, we don't even want to talk about times when we experienced lack. Don't tell others about past financial troubles until they are so far behind you that you can hardly remember how it felt. One who creates riches for him or herself opens a way for countless others to follow and inspires them to do so. Charity is good; it keeps people alive. However, inspiration can lead them out of poverty. Put poverty and all forms of lack and limitation behind you. You can make excuses, you can make money, but you can't do both.

The will is a determined purpose or desire, or an inclination that anyone can exercise, even a baby or a pet. My dogs have often 'willed' a piece of fish when I had no intention to share it with them. The will has power. Be certain of it or hold it to be true until you can't prove it wrong. Just as my dogs do not, you don't need persuasive or eloquent self-expression to will something and get a successful outcome. To ensure success, you need only to use your will power upon yourself. It is flagrantly wrong to impose your mental power upon others. Coercing with physical force is equally uncalled for. We cannot decide to do things for someone's 'own good', because we don't know what is truly good for others. Remember, manipulating others always backfires eventually, and when you reach that comfortable place, you won't want anyone trying to tear down your empire.

On the competitive plane, there is a godless struggle to gain power over others, but when we focus on creativity instead of competition, we open up unlimited possibility for everyone. Goodness can multiply where there is freedom, positive thought, enlightenment, and cultivation. Your will can be manifested when it serves others well.

Decide to be thankful and to live in gratitude.

Appreciation and thankfulness are the way to harmonious recognition and accepting all we desire. Many people who have taken every proper step to insure wealth fail because of their lack of gratefulness. Even a fool can prosper by acknowledging the wonder in the little bit he or she has. Love for what we have wills an impact on increase. This is applicable for any aspect of life. When we appreciate our friends, they want to be better friends, and the same is true with family. When we appreciate our bodies, we care for them and we improve physically. Even though money is a non-thinking substance, when we honor our own wealth, we don't tend to lose it through squandering or other seeming forms of loss. The respect you put forth will return in spades, even though we can't see its vibration in cash.

One of the first things to be grateful for is just possibility. No one is hopeless, and we all can create something outrageously successful, so we can be thankful for that. Having a deep and profound sense of gratitude for our chance to succeed is of the utmost importance. If you have any doubt in your mind that you have the same opportunity as others to succeed at something, your belief of lack will shut you down. Don't affirm that the Trumps or other moguls will have it all and you won't. Rich people have often lost all their money and more, and poor people have succeeded out of nowhere. You really have no lack or limitation, because there is nothing to which you cannot gain access to, that you need. You have everything you need right now, even if it's five bucks, 2 phone numbers and a pencil. There are no excuses. I started a television show without a big syndicator, being $600,000 in the red. With accounts receivable personnel calling us and a long-term payment plan, it was still possible. There is always a way. Never let excuses seem bigger than the vision.

Many people are kept in poverty by lack of gratitude. They cut their ties from what is good and by not acknowledging it, and it becomes a downward spiral from there. Appreciate what you have, even if it looks useless at this moment.

If your gratitude is strong and constant, the infinite Universe will give more of what you appreciate. Just as you receive friends when you give friendship, receiving all kinds of abundance is possible when you give thanks. The more living we appreciate, the more of life we'll be given.

If faith is still a challenge, it is born from gratitude. You can't make it without both so work these distinctions and they'll work for you.

Decide to advance with your vision.

No matter what profession or activity you choose, if you can enhance the lives of others and they appreciate your gift, they will be attracted to you, and you will find great success. The physician who holds the vision of himself as a great and successful healer and works toward this complete realization through that vision with faith and purpose will become phenomenally successful.

Increasing life or the quality of life is the way to funnel combined mental and personal action into an infallible state. If one wishes to advance in his present place or current job, he or she must work with gusto and enthusiasm. Do it with the idea of advancing for the sake of the self as well as the outcome that is to be achieved in that position. Hold the faith and purpose of improving during work hours, after work hours, and before work hours. Demonstrate it in such a way that every person who meets you will feel the power of purpose radiating from you. Everyone will also get the sense of advancement from you. People will be attracted to you, and if there is no opportunity for advancement in your present job, you will very soon see an opportunity to take another job.

Faith and purpose will allow anyone to quickly see any opportunity to better his or her condition. Never wait for an opportunity to be all that you can be. When an opportunity to be more than you are now is presented, and you feel impelled toward it, take it. This is just one more stepping stone toward a still greater opportunity. Self-actualization is available to anyone who can meet all of his or her needs and stay focused. I do not equate self-actualization, as Maslow meant it, and as Jung meant his term "individuation" as some kind of social or monetary success. Neither one of these men meant these things by the terms they used. Self-actualization is, ironically enough, a transcendence of "self" in the ego sense. It is a purely psychological achievement, having nothing at all to do with material success.

Material success is definitely admirable. An infinite number of valuable gestures have been done with money. These are powerful acts. It has been cited in the book, Critical Thinking in Psychology that people do not execute these gestures as selfless acts. People are basically selfish. Altruism is acquired through learning and experience. Proven in studies or not, improvements and generosity are appreciated in many ways, so power may be used for good, not evil. Many readers are seeking power, and regardless of the reason, power is attainable through these methods mentioned in this book.

It may not seem so, however, if people had this type of advancing mind and the faith that they could succeed, anywhere in the world, nothing could possibly keep them in poverty. Individuals who act in this way, at any time and under any government can make themselves rich. When a considerable number of individuals do so under any government, they will cause the system to be modified so as to open the way for others.

As we give no anxious cost to possible disasters, obstacles, panics, or unfavorable combinations of circumstances, it will be apparent that every difficulty carries with it the wherewithal for its overcoming.

Don't allow yourself to be led by others, jump onto their bandwagon and believe that your devotion to their ideas will allow you self-actualization. Sometimes people falsely feel as if they are saving the World, they become condescending and arrogant. This distinction comes from within you. Thinking the thoughts of others will not make you great. Following politicians and their causes classifies you as a lazy 'group thinker'. It doesn't show followers as great, but it can side track one away from the self-expression that would be truly fulfilling.

Never speak of yourself, your affairs, or anything else in a discouraged or discouraging way. Remember that words always have power. Never admit the possibility of failure. Never speak in a way that implies failure as a possibility. Never speak of times, such as a recession, or conditions as being doubtful. People have always found a way to succeed, and it is simply a function of faith that they have done so.

Never allow yourself to feel disappointed. Unfulfilled expectations may seem that a certain thing at a certain time has not been achieved. This does not constitute a failure.

Taking these steps will empower you like never before. You deserve to live your dream.

"Whatever your conscious mind assumes and believes to be true, your subconscious mind will accept and bring to pass. Believe in good fortune, divine guidance, right action, and all the blessings of life."

—Joseph Murphy

The Benefits of Empowerment

Your decisions will shine like diamonds. Needless to say, you will stay clear of trouble, become wealthy, and have the time of your life. You will be choosing from the cream on top instead of the bitter bottom.

The Implementation

This chapter is loaded with instruction, so write your mission statement and follow every outlined step to success.

The Cost of Living without Purpose and Empowerment

People rarely earn the type of money they deserve; this alone will taint your decisions. The majority don't live every day with passion. You will miss out on the most important decisions of your life.

The passion is within you, so let it flow and enjoy the ride.

**TECHNIQUES FOR
OTHER TYPES OF
DECISION-MAKING**

*There are circumstances where it is more difficult to use
the steps; the processes that fit those situations follow
in this section.*

GROUP DECISIONS

Corporations, associations, charitable organizations, schools and government, *and any other group entity* also make decisions. Of course, articulating a question to answer may be as important as the decision itself. Identifying issues before they become debilitating problems is a powerful function that protects the interests of the organization; it also strengthens and uplifts the entity.

Implementing change relies greatly on how the executives or members find potential issues to solve or purposeful modifications for betterment or growth. Finding the issue and framing it to contemplate the decision can make the entity weaker or stronger.

Friends make group decisions all the time. These decisions can be small, choosing where to go for dinner and what movie to see. They can have more moving parts and become complicated, like where to go on vacation. Mutual respect is an added implication that isn't such a consideration when making a decision for yourself. Certainly, when planning a birthday party, you will want to keep communications positive from the planning to the execution of the party.

Families also make decisions. Offering an empowered example for your children will not only influence the way they make decisions, but it will also allow them to create a life that brings joy, strength, and prosperity. It is also an imperative function of parents to demonstrate the type of behavior you wish to perpetuate in your children. If you don't want your children to be victims, don't demonstrate a victim consciousness, and please do usher in the ability to live an empowered life, ultimately raising successful adults.

"Don't handicap your children by making their lives easy."

— Robert A. Heinlein

Corporate entities have a flavor or a culture just as private families do. The way decisions are made can empower workers in a company to grow and become effective managers. Corporations with more at stake cannot afford to not keep it positive.

In any entity, effective leadership skills will yield better results from the decision to the implementation. Extraordinary leaders are effective problem finders as well as effective problem solvers.

A great leader does not fill the room with a bunch of 'Yes men.' It is wise to utilize opposing opinions and the experiences of other wise people. Capitalizing on the group enjoys a synergistic effort.

Conflict and debate are the greatest benefits that a group can provide. You have heard that two heads are better than one; if cognitive biases and groupthink are avoided, the devil's advocate can open the eyes of everyone to something unseen or not considered.

Optional methods to facilitate a decision

I believe that any truly important group decision can be made with all of the steps in this book. When I owned a TV production company in Los Angeles, it was not unusual for all of us to sit and meditate together and offer possible solutions. Available cash may decide many issues when the implementation reaches beyond the funds available, however listening to the ideas of the group can offer new ideas that fit well, even when applying all of the steps. New leaders can be identified when given the chance to shine.

Choosing an appropriate means of group interaction and undertaking a decision is as important as the implementation. How the decision is framed and explained will influence willingness to take risk, and the possible rewards will impact the efforts to be expended.

Now it becomes personal. What brings forth the most acceptable presentation for your group and considers the relevant factors in the most streamlined and manageable way?

There are times when a leader or business owner may not want much opposition. Other times leaders aim to include members of the group in discussion to placate members and make them feel valued. When you are looking for the absolute best solution for a high stakes issue, I do not recommend these options. Consulting multiple options and considering opposing viewpoints and alternatives will bring forth more details that are related. These simple processes can be less cumbersome for medium-to-small impact decisions:

<u>Unanimous decisions or rethink and postpone</u>

- Everyone has to agree on a given solution/proposition. When the unanimous decision does not come quickly, groups face the dilemma of having to dedicate more time than they hoped to make the decision or to have to change the decision-making process. The second option can lead to conflict and dissatisfaction, especially if only a small number of people in the group were "against" the majority.

- Putting off the decision until later might be the best decision at the time, but determining when the decision is needed, as well as the implementation, is key.

The Popular Vote Decides

- Everyone votes and a predetermined majority of the votes (i.e. 51%-100%) wins. The percentage of popularity the decision needs to carry must be decided by someone; this is the smaller decision, but can create discussion.

- Variations of this can also dictate the end result. 'Ranking' or 'Scoring' can yield a choice of set options or the 'yes' or 'no' to move ahead. Ask members of the group to rank the options if this applies, and adopt the highest-ranking option. Another method can be scoring on a scale and expecting a total point score or average point score (that is predetermined) to decide the issue.

Compromise for all

- This can go long and wide, with an effort to see everyone served in some relevant way. It will be key to avoid changing the original issue to decide, and to avoid unintended consequences (by trying to please everyone). Make a choice between option A or B. In the compromise situation, we would either look for a merge of A and B or collaborate to create a new option (C), but the original issue must be addressed and solved.

Consensus

- Implements a decision provided there is very little objection from the group. This usually involves the leader (or delegated person).

The process may look like this:

1. "This issue has been identified, and we would like to..."

2. "After careful consideration, I feel it can be done like this…"

3. "I would like to entertain discussion. Please share your comments, objections, and ideas by this (given) time and these (given) means."

4. The leader or a committee considers new input and can hone or accept the original decision as presented.

One person decides

- The leader or manager or another person with responsibility is often 'the one.' Some other person can also be delegated.

When one person decides and neglects the resources and ideas of other people, this is obviously suboptimal, especially if you are paying others to think. After learning about egocentrism and biases, it is hard to flush these out when the opportunity for this benefit is removed.

If an organization is always consistent with the way decisions are made, the member of the group (including employees) will understand and accept that being part of the group is to accept this process. This can be a time saver. Of course, employees may choose another place of employment, due to the offerings of that new company, and it is true that you can't please everyone. I concern myself with my personal ethics and allow others to choose for themselves.

There are infinite ways to come to a group decision, however, using all of this book's 7 steps as considerations for a group decision will inhibit a group from allowing many biases, individual inappropriate concerns, and selfish demands to take hold of the process.

Consequential factors for Group Decisions

When groups make a decision, they feel a polarizing force to accept greater risk than they would allow personally. It has been termed the **risky shift**. There may be a **neglect of probability** due to the use of other people's money, increasing some biases like the **cost sunk bias**.

Earlier, I mentioned the Ellsworth paradox. Don't forget that most individuals will prefer to avoid ambiguity. People prefer a game with known risks and rewards, and this extends into the real world, proving that most people prefer a job with a paycheck for a low standard of competent work over larger but unknown rewards for taking a risk. Offering ideas to a group injects risk that one's ego might want to avoid.

When a person has less to rely upon, individuals react to volatility, uncertainty, complexity, and ambiguity. People generally hate ambiguity and uncertain odds. Many studies found that poor odds are preferable over a game with uncertain odds. This is fascinating knowledge. Groups, conducted with strategy will be much more willing to risk to solve a problem. When you are leading a group, don't take the measure from your own shoe. They may feel a safety in numbers, or 'Groupthink' can take them in the opposite direction. Groups are not to be feared, but group dynamics are important to understand. It is certain that your output can be more valuable when you strategize your input.

"Boards today cripple themselves by not asking tough questions and allowing Groupthink to take hold. Fear of relevant feedback or criticism will block brilliant ideas and solutions."

–Michael Wickett

Avoiding the Dangers of Groupthink

Groupthink avoids conflict and smoothes over any possible disagreement on the team. Groupthink converges on only one idea that goes unquestioned and receives commitment without constructive opposition; this is often due to some perceived morality. Being part of the perceived altruistic or beneficial outcome halts any challenge to the idea. Sadly, the benefit of having many heads to solve an issue turns into a redundancy of one.

In the last chapter, I touched upon the weaknesses of the human mind regarding suggestibility and indoctrination. We must begin with strength of mind to make decisions. When we cannot rely on the metaphorical backbone to stand strong, not 'bending over,' we will miss, not finding the best solutions and making poor decisions that bring more challenges later.

Alexander the Great, Conqueror of the 4th century BC said, "I am not afraid of an army of lions led by a sheep; I am afraid of an army of sheep led by a lion." Groupthink is often dangerous.

To be certain that groups do not get lazy or try to make friends and alliances rather than find the best options (by using their own brains, skills, and point of view), it is important to separate opinions. There are many ways to do this.

1. Remove the boss from the room.

2. Encourage open dialogue by removing rules and order. Make every person equal and offer equal time.

3. Encourage skepticism instead of department cheerleading.

4. Brainstorm and demand an alternative from every member of the group.

5. Designate devil's advocates with the primary function to criticize.

6. Break the group into smaller groups to ascertain alternatives.

7. Consult with outside experts that hold no claim.

8. Ask lower level people (outside of the group) for their thoughts and also be certain to incorporate those who will implement this decision to be part of the decision process.

9. Demand that subgroups present an alternative rather than lazy agreement.

Always remember the old saying that *fools seldom differ.* More opposition can find better solutions. A great leader will find an empowering way to do this. Criticism from a devil's advocate does not have to bruise anyone's self-respect.

The 7 Steps and vigorous yet, empowering debate can yield the optimal decision. Praise for ideas and praise for criticism can offer a positive and crucial space to grow and find greater wisdom. Keeping the conflict constructive will allow psychological safety during criticism. Be certain those who step out with new thoughts are appreciated and feel valued.

Indoctrination is another enemy of decision-making.

This process instills and instructs a person with ideas, attitudes, strategies or methodologies without any critical analysis. This is dangerous to the subject of indoctrination because we are social beings that are shaped by cultural context, and the interjected beliefs may not serve the person being 'trained.' While parents and teachers are believed to be the major influences to indoctrinate, this detrimental process continues through the course of life, and our lazy, flawed brains allow it at all ages. Of course, the most susceptible are the youngest and oldest, but those who can learn to think and discern are hardest to indoctrinate. Beyond the vital function of forming stable communities, obeying laws and respecting others, people must think critically to overcome the ideas that are pushed by people who are self-serving or manipulative.

We have also touched upon several studies showing that at least 30% will agree even when they know better. They 'go along to get along' and don't have the necessary gumption to offer better ideas. Fear simply gets the best of them.

My undergraduate degree was in Business Administration. I studied to earn a Bachelors of Science, and this degree is now considered mostly obsolete or antiquated in the business World. My major was in Management. Even as I decree the obsolescence of so much knowledge, tests, and credit hours, people are now still the same. Humans are still using the same brain that performs similarly to the cave men of 300,000 years ago. I wish I could tell you that people are evolving, *I could hope so*, but don't allow people to surprise you *in the negative sense*. The studies I cite are valuable. I implore you to overpower human tendencies of the mind. Overcome these weak tendencies I mentioned, and you will see that it isn't as hard as it looks to succeed.

NO TIME FOR 7 STEPS? YOUR BEST IMMEDIATE DECISION STRATEGY

What if I need to act right now? Following 7 steps is great to buy a car or start a business, but what if you are in a rare instance, and there is no time? Your opportunity is right now, and every second counts. It is bound to happen, and your timing is not your choice.

When you find it absolutely necessary to make a decision and perhaps lives are involved in a very desperate or potentially harmful situation, you can do what the Navy Seals do; it is called **square breathing**. Before being killed or killing, rather than reacting incorrectly, a person can use this technique to become centered, calmer and less reactive, thus forming a better decision in the moment. Sometimes in life, we cannot wait to collect data and conduct a decision-making process; to do so might result in someone's death. Square breathing takes typically 16 seconds in textbook form, but this duration can vary longer or shorter, depending on the situation and person using it. I will describe square breathing and you can try it now.

Square breathing can be done in any physical position. Here are the steps that will center and calm you:

1. Breathe in for four seconds.

2. Hold this breath for four seconds.

3. Exhale this breath over four seconds.

4. Remain empty, without a breath for four seconds.

Being more centered is very beneficial. If you are desperate to make a decision, at least your mindset is improved. If you are on a battlefield, perhaps you have less than 16 seconds, reducing the time per step may be necessary. If you do this exercise as a 'mini meditation' for centering purposes, you can stretch each step longer, perhaps trying five seconds per step, and graduating to six second steps. Grounding yourself can allow you to make a better immediate decision.

Learning to 'think better' will also help anyone to make better overall decisions. Sadly, so often, people are driven in the moment to make very poor, illogical decisions. Also, people are manipulated to make choices that yield poor results. Embracing lessons of 'critical thinking' and logic can change your life and pave the way for the sum of your decisions to create a better quality of life for you. When you understand everything I offer in this book, you will be more confident and have greater knowledge to engage.

ADVANCED IDEAS AND TECHNIQUES

Decide to let go of that which doesn't serve you.

We have the power to decide what is important to us; this allows suffering to be optional. For some, it can become natural to feel sad, anxious, or angry. Without these daily annoyances, life might feel empty. Too many people allow these difficulties to become a crutch or an excuse as subconscious victim stories actually direct choices and behavior. It's easy to continue wishing that things were different, or the way we believe they ought to be. Alternatively, we can consider The Serenity Prayer; we need to know what we can and cannot change and from this realization move forward. Of course, it's arrogant to decide what's right for others, not considering their wishes. It's a waste of time to chase things and people who want something or someone else.

This will sound strange, but follow this train of thought. Fortunately, what we love or want can exist **without** importance- let me explain. Meaninglessness comes from the concept that we all feel differently about issues and perceptions of people, and to some, there is no importance. My best friend chooses not to celebrate her birthday, thinking attention is called to her age. Others want a big birthday party and lavish presents, *and God forbid anyone forgets.* I like to be pampered all day on my birthday, but I know I would have no problem surviving a birthday with a full day of work and cooking my own dinner.

One New Year's Eve, 20 years ago, I felt I had little to celebrate. That year I hadn't accomplished what I expected of myself and I wasn't sure if I wanted to stay home and skip the celebration. I was asked out for New Year's Eve, and I asked if he would mind pretending it was just a regular evening. He agreed, and we went to a fabulous restaurant, and had wonderful food and conversation aside from celebration. I felt no loss and had a good time. He wanted to spend New Year's Eve with me and was obliged, and I wanted to *not* celebrate and was equally served. Each of us got to frame it as we wished. Changing beliefs or reframing is always possible. It can be liberating, and increase what is available in our lives.

Some people pray before a meal. Some don't. Some eat monkey brains. Some don't. Some think watching football is a waste of time. Some don't. Some get married at age 12. Some wear wooden shoes. Some bring up their seventh son as a daughter. Some use cruel and unusual punishment. These beliefs are relevant to some and barbaric to others.

If a man believes a particular woman is one he can't live without, he is miserable when she doesn't want him. Perhaps 300 other men have met her and don't feel this way, knowing they prefer life without her. This particular man may *get to* change his mind and find happiness in another relationship. We hardly *have to* do anything, but we *get to* choose indifference or happiness rather than beating ourselves up.

People can make choices like this in a clear-cut, cold turkey manner. Wives that steam with anger while their husbands watch football could choose to occupy themselves with their own hobby or learn the rules of football and enjoy the game. Often open-mindedness spreads love, too.

Being set in our ways can put invisible walls in the path of what we want to create in our lives. With a negative attitude, we are unable to recognize good opportunities. We miss the doors that could be fulfilling opportunities when we have hostile thoughts running through our heads. I illuminated this because it's not necessary to remain unhappy. It's a waste of time to wish things were different when it's something you cannot control. Adults that feel a need to force other adults into their mold or their plan are stirring up trouble and losing out on the other more welcome and warm paths to experience. Unfortunately, far too many people do this in too many ways.

When we clear that space that had something uncomfortable occupying it, we are actually inviting something better to fill it. Take the round peg out of the square hole and look for the square peg. I think of my love life as a champagne glass. If beer is in the champagne glass, pouring champagne into it won't taste good. Clean out the beer and get the best vintage possible. We all deserve the best, whatever is good and uplifting in our lives.

We can find ourselves stuck in a complaint about the way life is; it's an annoying 'butt hook' and a recurring theme. I can redirect this behavior and offer a solution and good news. Basically, this recurrence constitutes operating on beliefs that are not true, and when I show this to a patient in therapy, they have no problem letting it go. They even laugh at themselves, but may also have a good cry before they walk outside to a new, happier world, free from the butt hook.

Do you have an ongoing 'complaint' that causes you to think or behave in a certain way to justify it? Justifying the behavior that is attached to it seems to work as an aid to cognitive dissonance. The purpose of getting perceived payoffs that are illusions, but subconsciously all of this transpires repeatedly. These negative notions are adopted and continue at an immeasurably large personal cost to oneself.

Are you making someone else wrong? Is their behavior irritating? Is it annoying to you? Are you doing or thinking something in response that band aids it for you?

Are you engaged somehow in what I call NONs? A NON is a Negative Obstructing Notion, *and it's worth nothing.* Since people are empty without these patterns that fill their days, we can replace them with something positive, and we can relieve the 'stuck' feeling that makes the 'NON' continue.

Without this 'NON' and the arrogance or arrogant responsive behavior that follows the complaint, anyone undoing a 'NON' can feel open, free, and live in a happier world, full of opportunity and joy. Suffering ends.

Create a belief to replace it. Make sure the new belief is true and empowering.

Here is a 'NON' example: *My spouse is trying to control me.*

The truth is that no one really controls other people. They can try to manipulate, but eventually manipulation fires back at the manipulator like a boomerang within a span of time. Learn to ignore it and they will cease to do it. Learn to rely on your thoughts and your choices and dismiss the need for others' approval. If you know you are doing great things, you will not need the approval of others.

As spats occur in response to such a complaint, it makes the complainer feel better to lash back. The truth is, as the pattern continues, it just gets messier and more unwelcome.

In a compassionate way, the 'NON' holder can ask forgiveness for anything that has been construed as poor communication, nasty, petty, or nagging behavior. Do not withhold any communication, but make sure everything you say comes from love *(not from blame)*; this pattern must be broken, and this must be done elegantly. Blame has a way of shutting off the other person's attention; the wall goes up. Share that something you did wasn't working and that you will take responsibility and offer a new promise or commitment. The other person must be heard first in order for this to be sincere. That means stay silent until they finish sharing. Do not interrupt or lose focus; hear the importance of their words. Explain that you are letting it go, and then believe more in being responsible than in being a victim.

Yes, somehow these 'NON's are subconscious beliefs that you are a victim. *This just isn't true.*

These 'NON's usually stem from childhood experiences rather than mature thinking that favors taking responsibility. 'NON's find a way to manipulate people and the environment rather than solving the issue or complaint in a responsible way. When we begin a 'NON', it is a defensive posture that is certainly powerless but feels justified and offers cognitive dissonance.

Say, *The Serenity Prayer* as often as needed. Live in the truth. Don't be a victim.

Decide to forgive and stop blaming.

When we can't forgive, we hold ourselves back. Forgiveness can certainly be done for the self instead of the one that has caused trouble or despair. You may believe that some people don't deserve forgiveness. This may seem very valid based on the facts, however, you hold yourself back when you are stuck on this issue. There comes a time to let it go so you can progress in life. I have written about many ways to forgive, so I hope you will research this and trust that letting go will allow you to go freely and focus on the intentions you want to create. A wise person once said, not forgiving is like drinking rat poison and expecting the rat to die. I think that sums up the cost of holding on to anger and blame. For now, realize that you must forgive and decide to do so now, so you can move on to better things in life.

"He who angers you conquers you."

~ Elizabeth Kenny

In essence, you allow others to control you and give them power over you when you hold onto blame. Reclaim your power with forgiveness.

Live with Purpose. Decide to express what you love.

No one has been denied a living or kept poor because opportunity was taken from him or her. In America, people can see this more clearly, but it is certainly true that energy is not lost anywhere in the Universe, even in the most underdeveloped countries. Again, wealth and success may be enjoyed in a way that may not be recognized by typical Americans. Money has never been fenced in by certain individuals. Monopolies of any kind are an illusion. There is nothing to stop us from expressing what we love.

Everyone on the planet has a talent. This is more than an axiom or maxim. It is a belief that can work for anyone. Accepting this will empower the believer or user instantly. Some people have many talents, but we all have something that can make us infinitely successful. We all embody gifts we don't have to doubt, and callings we might have worked hard to develop. The more we work with these gifts and callings, we find that we uncover more of our own talent and potential.

Practicing this chosen aptitude proves that there is always no limit to what can unfold, and more ability becomes evident which has previously been untapped. Anyone who works at their expertise daily for at least an hour, *or even better*, works to improve it as if their life depends on it, is guaranteed that in a reasonable time, it will bear fruit. You can be on a successful path to doing what you love as your profession. Your channels will grow. Superstardom is open for anyone in any area they are inclined toward. Of course, basic needs must be met first, lengthening the process. Abraham Maslow said that before anyone can even begin the journey to self-actualization, basic needs had to be met. It is often the case that people must ease the requirements of their lives by lowering their standards of living. This requires less time and money, allowing more to be given to the chosen path. One could drive a more economical car that is reliable, rather than making payments on an eight-year-old Mercedes for the sake of impressing others, *thus causing the need for extra responsibility instead of getting to work on one's purpose.* There are several things anyone can do to relieve stress and find more time, energy, and resources for developing something worthwhile.

Think about superstars in several areas. Examples may include musicians, basketball players, restauranteurs, software moguls, or designers of any kind. Things that they do outside of the realm where they excel are probably just ordinary. Michael Jordan had an awful time with baseball, and other troubles with golf, and these are all physical games. Kenny G won't be asked to play for the San Francisco 49ers. Cindy Crawford won't be asked to run a computer company. It is probably best to focus on one thing that brings us joy, knowing later it will bring others joy. There is an admirable path to success, even if not all people admire the talent that some appreciate. Not everyone is needed to share enthusiasm for an individual to enjoy success. Most people are unaware that Cindy Crawford was turned away early in her career by one of the biggest modeling agencies and told that she would never amount to anything with the mole on her face. To date, her success is undeniable, and she still exhibits the mole. Everyone has experienced rejection.

Experiencing rejection does not make us unique. What we do with the rejection can indeed make us unique. At the City of Hope, Cheryl Tiegs said to me in an interview that there is a positive experience to be had from every negative one. We were speaking of breast cancer at the time and finding 'silver linings' in disease is also possible. Rejection may always be painful for some. It is actually easier to simply be told 'no' with regard to receiving work than be left hanging with a 'maybe'. Be aware as much as possible of all opportunities. We all succeed eventually by knocking on the next door.

Superstars like Cher, Madonna, and Oprah demonstrated how being successful in one industry, can open doors to achieving even more success in other fields such as acting, book writing, and business. If for any reason you dislike any of these women, open your mind and consider this: These women are an inspiration because they know they have no limits. In exactly the same sense that they used this belief, you can too. It works universally for everyone.

Big success can come from anywhere, and no one will be able to stop it but him or herself. Dismiss this thought of limitation as quickly as possible.

What is your passion? What excites you enough to make you spring out of bed every morning? How can you pursue it? Make a list. Choose a talent on your list and plan to succeed at it. Be open to all channels when they present themselves and investigate their possibilities and consequences. Choose the channels that will take you where you want to be. Know that you will have to pay eventually for some calculated risks. Practice it, learn about it, and prepare every day.

There is a cost to resisting what you love. We are best at talents we develop and love. It can be the difference between each day dragging or flying by.

Define your mission and claim it.

For those who have already taken these steps, write a mission statement for yourself or your purpose or business. For example, this is mine--- *"My purpose is to provide empowerment for the unlimited possibilities for all people, including that which is optimal for the development of the body, mind, and spirit."* Mission statements can be changed throughout your life. They can also refresh our point of view about who we choose to be and what our priorities are when we refer back to them. **Inspire yourself with your personal Mission Statement.** Don't write it as if it will occur in the future. Use the present tense as I have with my example. This statement has been guiding me for over 25 years.

Clarify your mission as much as you can to keep yourself on track and personalize it to yourself.

For help writing the mission statement, go to **www.bestdecisionforyou.com/missionstatement**.

Look at your mission statement often. Read it at least once a day. Reading it in the morning and before you go to sleep is optimal. When you really know who you are, others will start to realize that you are a powerful and wonderful person.

Decide that work and earning money can be fun.

Life and work can be frustrating, especially around issues of money. Most of us approach work with typical American views; that life is a struggle to survive. Competition and hard work doesn't always payoff, money and property rights come before health and human rights, and some people are perceived as more valuable and deserving greater pay and perks. Approaching life as a battle makes it seem exhausting, like it's some kind of race, or game we can't win. These thoughts are derived from a core belief that we are separate from everyone else. By seeing ourselves as separate, we tend to perceive people and circumstances as more powerful than we are. Fortunately, this is not true.

Because business is an overwhelming part of society and many people are dependent on their incomes, it is important to clarify the role of business and the support it brings to our lives. We are each a perfect and essential part of a large picture that continually grows in size and beauty. Whenever any of us connects with our true greatness and expresses it, countless others can receive the joy derived from it. All forms of work are also enhanced by putting in additional effort and implementing ideas. Think of software, furniture, and the utility companies, for example.

Business has the potential to be an outlet for loving, supportive, and creative opportunities. Abundance is facilitated by creativity.

Each of us can feel free to express this glowing part of ourselves. This is characterized as purpose or vision for those who have identified it in themselves. We can then add to the abundance of everyone on the planet. It benefits us all to be supportive in helping others express their brilliance. We can create a thriving environment and be supportive of others. These efforts come back, as givers are always receivers.

It is essential to understand that money follows, it does not lead. Whenever money is expected to lead, there are chaotic results. If there is any doubt, check out the trouble dollars cause everywhere, including lines and service at the largest banks.

Before you quit your day job, it's important to know that responsibility for your obligations, such as rent or mortgage payments and the like, are important, but also using your talents to do something with purpose in this world is also your responsibility. You have been given talents for a reason. Talents are also learned, and when you have passion for your purpose, you must not ignore it. In many ways, you are blaspheming the Great Spirit that offered this divine idea and purpose when you do not act on it. You may need to ask yourself several questions to see if your heart is in the right place. If your heart is in the right place and your purpose taunts you every day to perform, a lack of money, lack of talent, or lack of knowledge cannot stop you. An overwhelming population does not know a purpose in their souls. It is a blessing to be clear and to allow this self-expression to flow through you. Your purpose is an inspired gift, and you will have true power if you are co-creating with the Infinite. If you do not believe in a Power greater than yourself or a Creator, belief in yourself can be enough to bring your idea into manifestation, so let's take that test. We are all spiritual beings, whether we believe this or not, and the same Universal rules will work for anyone. You need not believe in gravity for it to work on you, and this is the same property.

Your heart will take you to fruition if you have identified a void in the Universe and a solution is wanted by humanity and consumers. If you can cause enough consumers to buy your product or service, you will be financially successful with your divine idea. The value of your idea is to enhance the lives of others; it is not everyone's goal to be rewarded financially. If the unintended consequences caused by your divine idea are too great, there will be pushback and obstruction from those you potentially hurt.

Relatedly, if you can be *for* something that can be defined with spiritual qualities rather than against something, Universal principles will rush to open doors. *What do I mean by this?* Does your idea pass the Mother Theresa test? Mother Theresa said, "If you are having an anti-war rally, I will not come, but if you are having a peace rally, I will be there." Reverend Dr. Martin Luther King, Jr. has in his words agreed with this premise. Peace is a spiritual quality. If your idea offers others a quality like prosperity or joy or beauty, you are on a positive path. There are many more spiritual qualities from health to love that are all wanting to be expressed by humanity and consumers. If you have more questions about spiritual qualities, please visit
www.bestdecisionforyou.com/affirmations or
www.bestdecisionforyou.com/qualities.

Decide to claim your birthright.

I mentioned that a lack of funds, information or talent will not hold you back. Explanations of such claims are here, in the text. It is everyone's right to be rich, including the wealth of money and possessions. If this is not so, how could so many individuals go from rags to riches, and why can others follow in their success? There is no reward in having less than what you want. Any individual who can't afford all that he wishes for may not be living to his or her full potential. It is also true that no individual is worthier than another of having financial success.

Reasonable people typically enjoy creating a comfortable home, reliable automobiles, and giving gifts at appropriate times of the year. These common intentions can be difficult or impossible when earning money is challenged. In addition, when we feel we are coming up short, our self-esteem takes another dive. This is definitely a very Western point of view that is spreading. Wealth and poverty are demonstrated throughout humanity, but experienced differently in other cultures in which wealth is perceived in a different way. The same is true for business. Reasonable standards can be maintained to keep the business aligned. We prefer to keep loyal and hardworking employees rather than denying them a well-deserved raise. Employees may need insurance, company cars, and other perks, and will join another organization if they feel they are getting less than their worth. These challenges are stressful and can be debilitating.

The biggest frustration in expressing love is the sting of poverty. It's often not feasible to quit your day job when you are pursuing dreams. It can be a difficult dance for a while, but people who express their purpose are less frustrated with life and can find meaningful human relationships and good health.

If anyone chooses to avoid success in the self-actualization or financial senses, they are hurting themselves and the rest of the world. This will eventually become clear; however, you can render humanity (or God if you prefer) no greater service than to make the absolute most of yourself. For those who fear God, God is not the least bit pleased with sacrifices, poverty, or wasting any of the gifts and potential that has been given. No one will be canonized for not earning all he or she can.

We live for the body, mind, and soul. Each is desirable, and none are unimportant. There is no nobility in living only for the soul and neglecting the body. Not caring for your body is disrespectful to the self and all others. It is equally sad to live for the intellect and neglect the body and soul. Troubles always come to those who neglect to take care of all aspects of their life. Those who don't care for their bodies will be met with prejudice and disrespect. The spirit unfolds in the freest way when worries of health, intelligence, and money don't exist.

Every individual has something to contribute to all who live in the world, but can give more to the richness, power, elegance, and beauty when he or she isn't part of the problem. The best thing one can do to aid the impoverished is not to be poor. This is a strong premise, enunciated in a speech by Reverend Dr. Martin Luther King.

To be a giver is the most rewarding experience we can express. Earning substantial funds and property allows one to bestow benefits on those he or she loves. Giving is a reward. Self-esteem is strengthened by giving. The position of giving makes one feel powerful. Decide to positively influence others.

No matter how you do your purpose or business, it is necessary to convey the impression onto others that they will experience an increase by working with you. This is not to 'toot your own horn,' but it is to enroll them into your vision. This can be done on the phone, in person, on the internet, or probably any possible way we can communicate.

The desire for increase is inherent in all people, and in all nature. All men and women are attracted to the person who can give them more means to enjoy life. Promote to advance mankind and convey advancement in all social situations as well. More doors will open for you.

Since true faith is never boastful, bragging is unnecessary. When you meet a boastful person, you know you are meeting someone who is secretly doubtful and afraid. Being arrogant, haughty, conceited, or pretentious will not work on your behalf for very long. Always come from the heart, expressing how you can help others. The intuition of others will be aware of this sentiment.

While influencing others, we must avoid the temptation to gain power over others. We must only have control over ourselves, because all else is an illusion. In creating master/slave relationships, there is a price to pay later, and it may set you back past your starting point. Ultimately, you will never control anyone but yourself. This is always evident in the end.

Your efficiency will be noticed and earn more business for you. It can come from places unexpected or unknown. Remember, it is not actually the number of things you do each day, it is the efficiency of each action that has been done. Then the question becomes, *can I make every step or every action efficient?* Yes, you can. Hold your vision while accomplishing each task. Make every action a strong one, never coming from weakness or fear. Acting without faith can certainly cause failure. Without being showy, demonstrate your proficiency with confidence, not with conceit. Threatening others will not attract them to participate with you. The perception of others is key for most businesses. Others must discern that you will help them, increase their value, or gain for them what they desire to increase. That memorable line in the movie, Jerry Maguire says: "Help me to help you."

Decide to find the right business or be the founder of a useful organization.

In order to succeed, you must possess a well-developed state of faculties required for that job or vision. We have all seen extremely talented people that have achieved no success. The different faculties are tools, which are essential to use in the correct way. Good tools alone do not assure success.

It is important to use your strongest faculties---the one for which you are naturally 'best inclined.' There are also limitations to this statement. Do not limit your vocation as being irrevocably fixed by the skills with which you were born. Talent can also be developed.

Rudimentary talent may allow you to succeed in any vocation, and there is no talent of which you have not at least a small amount.

You can succeed most easily if you do that for which you are best fitted. However, you will get rich most satisfactorily if you do that which you want to do. Desire is a manifestation of power.

Success at anything can be a bumpy road. Don't be afraid to make a sudden and radical change if the opportunity is presented and if you feel, after careful consideration that it is the right opportunity. Never take a sudden or radical action when you are in doubt. Mistakes come from acting hastily, or acting in fear or doubt, or in forgetting the right motive. In other words, to combine many ideas, do all that you can do in a perfect manner every day, but do it without haste, worry, or fear. Go as fast as you can, but never hurry haphazardly.

Decide to increase the quality of life for others.

Because every person exists to be a consciously living being, enlightened with this belief or not, each person possesses somewhere within him or herself the natural and inherent desire of every living intelligence for the increase of life. Every living thing must continually seek for the enlargement of its life, because life, and the mere act of living, must increase in itself. Just as a seed dropped into the ground, it springs into activity, and in the act of living produces 100 more seeds. Life, by living, multiplies itself. It is forever becoming more, because it must do so to continue to exist.

Intelligence is governed under this same necessity for continuous increase. Every thought we think makes it necessary for us to think another thought. Consciousness is continually expanding. Every fact we learn leads us to learning another fact. Just as knowledge is continually increasing, every talent we cultivate brings to the mind the desire to cultivate another talent. This process continues, and in seeking expression for this urge, we are compelled to know more, to do more, and to be more.

Having purpose, in essence, is seeking fulfillment. It is life, seeking fuller expression. Life is permeated with the desire to live more. This is why we create things. We always want to have things we can use to increase life, and to be a greater expression of our purpose, desires, and vision.

Because the Universe is friendly, nature is friendly to our plans. You may be certain that this is true. It is essential, however, that your purpose must harmonize with the purpose that is in everything. It is necessary to want real life, not mere pleasure for sensual gratification. Just as getting rich in order to live swinishly for animal desires is not aligned with perpetuating life, enjoying mental pleasures, including the increase of knowledge to outshine others, or to be famous are not a part of surveying one's purpose. A person who creates an empire for these reasons will never be satisfied with his earnings. High ideals such as Dharma are not embodied by these desires.

There is nothing wrong with achieving wealth so that you can eat, drink, and be merry when it is time to do these things. Seeing distant lands, feeding your mind, and developing your intellect are all parts of living in your purpose.

In order to be successful, there is no necessity to take anything away from anyone. It is not necessary to drive sharp bargains. Cheating and taking advantage will only impair success. Others need not work for you for less than he or she is worth.

We must all realize, for the sake of humanity, that supply is unlimited. Never look at the visible supply. Always look at the limitless and infinite abundance of natural beauty and accomplishment. Of course, this is much easier for an American who hasn't missed a meal, so Step One for some is to get *any* job, *even if it is sweeping floors*. Aside from babysitting, my first official job was checking toes for fungus in a Park District Pool locker room. It wasn't the least bit glamorous. It paid lousy, but it was a stepping stone to be a lifeguard, and this happened much faster than the boss intended. My license, attitude, and readiness to take that lifeguard chair transformed my title within 30 days, and my teenage dream came true.

See a flower for the perfection that it is. There will always be a way to succeed with a divine idea without depleting the planet. Do not allow yourself to think for an instant that all the best building spots will be taken before you get ready to build your house. Always remember that the supply of all that you need is limitless, so no one will 'beat you to it'.

An empowered decision can empower others. Your decision has exponential power.

Decide to prioritize.

Being successful is exciting and creates many questions. Prioritizing will become necessary to create or sustain success with your relationships, health, and finances.

With so many choices and so much to do, you will need to get organized. You will become proficient at making lists. You will benefit by making a list of all the things you would like to do every day. Many time managers suggest assigning an A, B, or C to every item on the list. A's are the most important to do that day. C's are somewhat important but could wait until tomorrow. You will accomplish your A's first, your B's second, and if you are really organized and the stars line up properly for you that day, the C's may also get crossed off the list. If any items on that list are not completed, you can write them on the next day's list. It is possible that a C can become an A in coming days. Get it? Working without a "to-do" list is risky. I recommend adhering to this practice immediately if you have not already.

Decide to take prioritizing to an advanced level.

I find it valuable to add five things I can do to work toward the completion of my latest goal to my list daily. This practice helps to move progress forward rapidly. Try it when you are ready for *the big time.*

Decide to have high self-esteem.

All I can tell you is low self-esteem is a lie. You really are good enough. You have not been given an inclination without a means to achieve it. Many times, when you succeeded, you didn't allow others to stop you. Why let thoughts derived from the past stop you now, *or ever?* You have come through many times, and the bottom line is, you are worthy, just like anybody else. We have all lied to ourselves, and whatever it has cost you—time, money, a loving relationship, or the health that you also deserve—forget it. Let it go and get accustomed to believing that you are just as equal as any other citizen. This is your truth, granted by the Constitution of the United States of America or God, whichever you prefer. You have the right to pursue happiness, just like any enviable, successful person you have ever heard of. In this world we can change things in a minute. In this world of change, go ahead and make a commitment to seeing yourself in a bright light every day. Smile and hold your head high. Attract happiness with your joy and appreciation for life. It really works. I swear life is good. All you have got to do is believe it. Hold it as your truth. It will work for you as it has for me.

If you don't see your value, know that you have been lying to yourself. I can't imagine what you may have lost if you subscribed to beliefs that you are not worthy or able enough to succeed in life. Change your mind. *Change your life.*

> *"It is almost impossible to be consistent with your goal if your subconscious mind is constantly fed with negative perceptions of its road."*
>
> ~ Edmond Mbiaka

Decide to embrace failure if it occurs rather than being stagnant.

The people that accomplish the most also fail the most. Always remember that we 'fail forward' and can choose to call it experience.

When we fail, we learn what doesn't work and other paths to probable success tend to show up. If you knew you would eventually succeed, would you fail several times?

Consider failure as feedback. Feedback is also valuable. Remember, your vision is in front of you; it is your guiding light. Remember daily to feel what it would feel like if you succeeded and allow that feeling to guide you to the next step. If you don't have a vision, circumstances will guide you and you will become reactive instead of the proactive being that you are meant to be. Most of us don't have to lead 24 hours a day but knowing that your divine idea needs you to uphold it, you can accept the responsibility and the rewards. Every being must claim the power and the purpose within himself or herself.

None of us have always made the right decisions. You can look back at your life and find a few you might love to change. You may have learned a lesson, or perhaps that experience is best explained as an opportunity to go back and apologize for something. Do what you can, and have the wisdom and integrity to recognize what you can change.

"Sometimes you make the right decision; sometimes you make the decision right."

~ "Dr. Phil" McGraw

Decide to stack the deck against the poor decisions/direction of others.

Feel like you already own what you desire. We're not talking about exaggerating or lying about what you have or who you are. Confidence, posture, and appearance will work on your behalf to put you in a position to get what you want. The rest is up to you.

Attitude and self-assurance will project into others opinion about you. Simply appearing to know where we are going can save us from conflict. On a dark city street, any criminal element will choose to attack someone who looks lost and lacks confidence. That person has the appearance of any easy mark.

I've been attacked four times in my life. I became angry and tired of being a victim. I decided to stop parting with my possessions and stop spending time replacing credit cards. After careful speculation of a few schools, I enrolled in a karate class. Without trying, I acquired the look of confidence and peacefulness. I gained discipline that I hadn't exercised since college. I learned the "soft eye", a tremendous technique for awareness. It's looking at the opponent without seeming focused on what his hands and feet are planning. To defend myself, I learned to encompass vision all around me. Walking down a dark city street, it's better not to turn your head nervously or awkwardly. We benefit by knowing who and what is around us. In a potentially dangerous place, while feeling closed in like a bug that's about to be squashed, I assuredly turn to the one that puts off the ambiguous vibes and ask a question. "What time is it?" No one has ever believed I was afraid following that. If a victim was attacked, it wasn't me.

Within six years, I became a black belt. Many years ago, at around 2 P.M. in L.A., I stood by my car waiting for AAA to come and jump-start it. A man in his 20's walked up to me and showed me his knife. I said, "Nice knife. Are you sure you can take me?" He was taken back. The tow truck arrived a minute later, and I was happy there was no physical confrontation.

Simultaneous to the knife incident, my ex-husband was at a gas station four miles away. After filling his tank, he attempted to get into his car and leave. A young man put a gun to his head and asked him to get out of his car, and give him his wallet. Within a second my ex hit the young man with his door, knocking him to the ground. He instantly drove off as the young man rose up and began shooting. My ex had taken karate for a little less than a year, but developed the reflexes he needed in that situation to get away with his car and life. *It wasn't a smart chance to take, but amazingly it worked.*

The point here is to be aware at all times. When we are confident with our physical level, mechanics, technique, academics and the psychological aspects of the task, then the calmness of the spiritual level will guide us, and we will flow with our actions, as effortlessly as Michael Jordan made his baskets.

In karate, like any physical task, we can flow with grace and ease when we utilize the three elements of speed. These concepts become second nature. The first is relaxation. That's why we often take a deep breath before difficult endeavors.

The second is explosiveness. This is the conviction we employ, which pulls us forth with momentum. The third is independent movement. This can be described as each movement executed correctly. The Three Elements of Speed are beneficial even at times we don't want to appear speedy, such as stand-up comedy or job interviews.

Martial Arts can be very helpful in attaining confidence, and bring students into peace and spirituality. Always choose a sensei (teacher) with great credentials and genuine qualities; unassuming and humble. It is a wonderful workout for the mind and body. It is also likely to bring about enlightenment.

It isn't necessary to enroll in karate to be a success; however, it will change your life.

This point is to have poise and to be comfortable in all situations, never seeming incapable or victim-like. Appearing desperate, afraid, or shifty can crush an opportunity. The more confidence we have in the way we present ourselves, the more we ease business and personal relationships. We attract what we are. How we perceive ourselves can raise the echelon where we live. We can always remember that and count on the results. So, don't complain, because misery loves company.

Decide to appear confident.

Posture is one thing you can change instantly to demonstrate a more attractive, secure, and reliable appearance. It immediately improves anyone's look, as the chest looks prouder and younger, the spine and neck look healthy, and larger shoulders create a smaller looking waist and hips. It displays confidence- others can think well of you. It exhibits happiness, which attracts happiness. If you want others to care for and respect you, consider putting your shoulders back, and your chest out. No one will want to treat you better than you treat yourself.

"Always practice competently with confidence and intelligence and the subconscious mind will eventually accept it as your norm."

~ Parul Agrawal

Decide to surround yourself with a circle of positive people.

The human psyche is somewhat predictable. You will take on the traits, positive or negative of those who are closest to you. Be careful to decide with whom you will spend time. Some say, life is short, and we realize this as we get older. Even more importantly, your quality of life depends upon this premise. If you act like the people you socialize and work with, is this healthy for you? We are permeable people. We are not Teflon and we are physiologically and psychologically changing all the time. Consciously, if asked, do you want to change for the better or the worse? Each of us must be conscious of this and make this decision. Your entire quality of life is influenced greatly. Do you want to be lazy and complain or do you want someone to raise the bar for you and be your cheerleader?

If you want to operate in a circle of light, choose it. Also know that people that are attractive and successful won't want to be around a sulker or complainer, and you can be dumped, so rise to the occasion whenever possible. No one is perfect, but you will be happier with your life if you raise the bar and fill the space with positive energy.

Oprah recommends surrounding yourself with people who are going to lift you higher, and Tony Robbins says you actually become the people with whom you spend your time. If there is a chance to be with their friends, I would strongly advise it. Imagine for a moment, which empowering authors would you like to be your friends? You can spend some of your 'alone time' enriching and empowering yourself. Recharge your 'batteries.' Sometimes I take my "friends" in the car and listen to empowering audio books; I read and learn often, and I find this uplifting.

Are Your Antennas Up?

Here is a decision that you get to make. (You noticed I specified, "get to" instead of "have to" and I will complete that thought shortly.) Here is your dilemma: You will receive the gift of a free automobile. You can pick any automobile you want, but here's the catch...it's the ONLY automobile you will ever have. Now, I am sure you are thinking, *I will need to take very good care of this automobile*. Absolutely. You WILL need to take very good care of this automobile. Here is the real story: *You have received a vehicle, and you only are allowed one;* **this is your amazing, human body**. How do you decide to care for your vehicle? Do you keep your body in good condition? Do you feed it properly and treat it in a manner that will allow your body to last a lifetime? Do you remember to exercise? Are you feeding it with low grade fuel or healthy food? Do you overfeed it and weigh down your vehicle in ways that will stress your joints (like your knees) also stressing your organs and increasing your risk of cancer and other diseases? I could go on and on listing the detrimental results we cause as we drive our vehicles carelessly. Actually, I heard a speaker or two offer this dilemma to audiences, and this is not an original line of thought. I deeply appreciate it, as I am an international speaker, and I have had the luxury of hearing a multitude of great speakers. The point is, why don't we do more to care for the only vehicle we will ever have? When we think about it, we realize that perhaps less than 1% of people are really acting on this decision as if their life depends on it. Truly, your life and my life *do* depend on it. Why do we fail to make good decisions throughout the day? This question certainly brings value to this book. Unfortunately, we need to see these little decisions as a process rather than an event, like dinner. Instead of seeing dinner as an event, we need to see it as an opportunity to make good choices, which is actually an ongoing process. When we decide to wake up and be fully conscious, we can improve our decision-making and lives, which will be measurably better. I am telling you that being 'results oriented' will help you to become a better decision-maker. If I use this "vehicle" logic and narrow it down to eating or fueling your body, I am reminded of Nikki Haskell, a celebrity icon and entrepreneur. Nikki was a guest on my network TV show, Infinite Power. Nikki was the only guest who wore high heels with her gym clothes on 4 years of this show; let me tell you, she was a hoot. Anyway, Nikki said that for those who wanted to lose weight, simply eat in front of a full-length mirror, in the nude. *If that doesn't bring your focus into a clear picture, I am not sure what could.* People mindlessly eat cookies all day. Would you eat the cookie if you were nude in front of a mirror? Please consider that. So many little choices measurably affect our lives. We must focus our minds and engage in a results-oriented manner. This habit of casually eating a cookie whenever we pass one can add up to obesity or diabetes in time.

To be clear, the keys to fuel your mind and influence your decisions are *conscious process and results.* Sleepwalkers lose.

In our daily lives, we find ourselves in a position where we "have to" go to work, "have to" take a shower and get dressed, eat a meal, and the list could go on endlessly. The truth is, you don't have to go to work. You have made a choice to go to work, based on earning money to afford the things you need and want. You don't have to take a shower. You could stink all day and see what that causes, including skin conditions, lack of friends, and social disgrace. You get to pick up your kids so that no harm will come to them, and because you wanted those kids, those kids mean something to you, and hopefully you love them dearly and make the best decisions when you raise them. Almost all of life is a "get to", and there are very few have to's, like dying. With this logic, you don't have to pay taxes. You get to, so that you will not be punished like a criminal. As you can see, everything is a choice, and this usually includes when you die, to some extent, depending very much on your decisions.

With all of this said, WAKE UP. A wise person once said, your life is not a dress rehearsal. Live the best you can, and whatever you do, don't be one of those sleepwalkers. (And God Bless Nikki Haskell.)

Are You Up For Life?

In the last section, I spoke of Nikki Haskell and how she was sharing a secret to weight loss with my TV audience of millions. This reminds me of a story about the very inspiring Famous Amos. Years before I had my own TV show, I was working as a spokes model at McCormick Place in Chicago. I met Famous Amos, the chocolate chip cookie magnate. I have to assume that it was a food show I was attending, but this was 30 years ago. The FMI-Food Marketing Institute was a yearly trade show at McCormick place. I was a spokesmodel for Kraft Foods and worked year after year for Kraft as a game show host, playing a game with grocery store executives and owners. I distinctly remember speaking with Amos (his real name is Wally) in his booth. Of course, I wanted to meet famous Amos. You already know how I love chocolate. As we spoke, I noticed that he was playing with something in the front pocket of his pants. I asked him what he was playing with, and a moment later he pulled it from his pocket to show me. I saw a wad of crumpled paper and asked what significance it had. Wally told me that he kept it in his pocket to remind him to elevate his enthusiasm to a level 6 times higher than what he was feeling. I paraphrase this for you now. At that moment, it resonated as a good idea, but on that day, I didn't realize it was a true secret to success in life. I can't tell you the significance of "6", but that is what he said, and I am not sure how you can be six times more excited rather than 5 or 7 times more excited. The bottom line is that moping around and slumping will get you NOTHING. With enthusiasm for his product, at his best, it has been reported that Famous Amos was selling $10,000,000 of cookies per year. I heard Famous Amos Cookies was acquired by Keebler, owned by Kellogg's. In my recollection of meeting Wally Amos years ago, I can distinctly remember our conversation about a wad of paper, and I am happy to share this concept with you. Making a decision to be happy and enthusiastic is a wise strategy.

Sulking is just horrible; you do not want to be seen sulking. If you are a very introverted person and want to try some positive vibes, just smile all day and be happy toward everyone you meet. You will probably get invited to something interesting or fun. This happens to me all the time. Everyone looks better when they smile. If you want a friend, be a friend. Be positive. Everyone looks terrible when they sulk. Slumping, muttering, whining, complaining and the like cannot help you; it can only hurt you.

Enthusiasm takes energy; this is why people don't subconsciously choose to get excited. The human body is programmed with the tendency to preserve energy for when it's needed. Do you have to sell something? Do you sell yourself at work, socially, or have a cause worth enrolling others? Do you need to be emotional or get "pumped up' at the gym to work out? Radiating positive energy can help you as well as connect you to others. Enthusiasm is contagious.

Enthusiasm is an energy that amplifies your drive. It will sustain you through all the ups and downs and become your differentiator and recipe to success.

~ Deborah Bateman

Are you Grateful for Life?

Hard to believe in my world, but so many people don't understand what a true advantage gratitude brings into any life. There are so many books written to bring gratitude into your life that I will not explain it fully. If you are not starting your day positive, in gratitude, start now, *or get one of those books.*

Decide to appear for what you want to receive.

Most people will judge the clothing and outward appearance of others. They see someone and form a first impression before a word is spoken. Be sure that who you claim to be and your intentions are properly portrayed by the presentation you choose.

Women might consider not wearing a revealing outfit on a first date, as the date will think she is hoping to have sex, *unless that's the real intention*. It's rather hard to form a connection that is more than physical when the attire is so distracting. Sexy supermodels and actresses who date rock stars can pull it off, but don't try it at home, unless you are seeking heartbreak. Remember, we rarely hear that rock stars are faithfully devoted to their soul mate. Men believe that if you show them sex, that's the purpose of the date. If you want to show off a great shape, wear something form fitting, *but not naked*. Too much bare flesh across the table will prevent him from hearing anything serious you want to say.

Work is a time for proper attire. Ask questions if there is any uncertainty regarding dress code at your place of employment. I've noticed that there's a fine line drawn in seemingly similar consulting firms, among other businesses. At certain firms, beautifully tailored Italian suits with clean crisp monogrammed shirts accompany a stylish silk tie. Cuff links give the added indication of a knack for detail. On the other hand, others exhibit a more classic tone. The ultra-conservative Brooks Brothers style seems the norm. They show their colors in a conformist way.

Body piercing and purple hair do not prove that people are individuals. Generally, it is more of a show of lack of ways to be self-expressive. Few industries and some people will exhibit such details and it is perceived appropriate. When we can express ourselves from our hearts, coming from love, a greater impression or impact will be made. A multitude of body piercings are radical, and would be construed as a statement of wanting to be separate from most others, unless you own a piercing store. Success is never going to be achieved by highlighting separation. People subconsciously like others similar to themselves. Don't be naïve enough to think that you are not being judged at all times; *it may not be right*, but this will continue to be.

Wearing dirty clothes or scuffed shoes are messages to others that one either: a) doesn't care, b) doesn't have good hygiene or isn't clean, or c) lives at a poverty level. *Would you date or hire someone like this?* It's the same for ladies with chewed up heels on their shoes. It's unlikely that a messy person would have the same opportunities as a well-presented person. Jackie O. wouldn't have gone so far covered in tattoos. That is not to say that all women want to marry the President of the United States or billionaires. *There is no right or wrong about appearances, only the consequences society dishes out.*

Honestly, it pains me to bring up appearances at all, but **not** offending others is important when enrolling people into your plans for anything you value. It seems obvious, however I have witnessed failures caused by this issue alone. If they don't care for you, blaming them will not bring you closer to your goal.

Others hear ideas and visions more clearly when your appearance isn't shrieking at them. Trying something more mainstream is never a bad experiment. Improving one's appearance might also gain more attention, as long as it's classic. Traditional colors for hair, make-up, and fingernails *are beautiful* and safer.

Most plans have a better chance of being adopted when others are comfortable and trust you. Be appropriate and confident for any important situation. Appearing overdone, dirty, or too trendy for the latest fashion magazines will reduce your effectiveness, as communication is minimized.

A PERSONAL DECISION FOR SUCCESS THAT CAN BEAT THE ODDS

Is this you? "I did my research and calculated the risks. My experience is not an asset. I'm 'green,' but itching to do it anyway.

I can lose big, but every part of me wants to start now. *Can I make it?"*

What supersedes unfavorable, factual data with a desire to say YES when the odds don't look good? Here are two concepts that have merit:

- Your will, your clearly defined purpose, your attitude, passion and effort

- Mysticism, including universal laws, physics, metaphysics, quantum physics, and grace

The first answer will open your mind and heart. My second answer may send you into thoughts that disagree, including thoughts that this is just too 'airy fairy.' Is Einstein airy fairy?

"The finest emotion of which we are capable is the mystic emotion. Herein lies the germ of all art and all true science. Anyone to whom this feeling is alien, who is no longer capable of wonderment and lives in a state of fear is a dead man. To know that what is impenetrable for us really exists and manifests itself as the highest wisdom and the most radiant beauty, whose gross forms alone are intelligible to our poor faculties – this knowledge, this feeling ... that is the core of the true religious sentiment. In this sense, and in this sense alone, I rank myself among profoundly religious men."

~ Albert Einstein

Oddly, emotions play a huge role in both. When thinking critically, we need to put emotions aside. Mysticism and your will are best aroused with enthusiasm. There is no good decision made when you are angry, but when you are happy and excited, that is where this chapter gains its power.

Good news ensues. Without believing in mysticism and metaphysics, you can enjoy the benefits anyway. If you can focus on my advice and stay positive, the laws and physics will be at your tail and push you forward. It really is that simple, but you are a complicated and complex being, and you will need to clear your ego and biases. There is a winner in all of us. You can do it. You may need some troubleshooting for challenges and your blind spots.

> *"Our subconscious minds have no sense of humor, play no jokes and cannot tell the difference between reality and an imagined thought or image. What we continually think about eventually will manifest in our lives."*
>
> ~ Robert Collier

This quote is great in the same way that the book and movie, The Secret is valuable. The criticism that I hear most often with The Secret is that we hear all about focusing on what we want, *but how do we get it? Does a genie bring it one day?* The short answer is no. There is a saying that comes to mind that I learned at Agape Spiritual Center in Los Angeles, and I have been saying it ever since the first time I heard it 27 years ago.

Treat and move your feet. **Treat** means to affirm what we will accomplish, who we will be and what spiritual qualities we will express, and also our gratitude and certainty of its manifestation. It is an **affirmative prayer**. This is our focus, and we trust in God that it happens, because we say it is already done in the mind of God.

Move Your Feet is the missing step in The Secret. If you knew it would happen and were certain, you would advance without fear.

You would take the steps necessary to express this divinity that is clear to us when we treat for it.

Treatments are very individual, although any being would want to express love, health, abundance, compassion, peace, joy, and of course, more than that.

Doing an affirmative prayer is like doing affirmations on steroids. An atheist can do affirmations without any conundrum. If one doesn't believe in a Creator, some of the steps may be challenging, but I think it's possible to get around these quandaries. When I 'treat' for myself or others, I affirm God's existence. This would be a challenge for atheists. The second of the 5 steps, is to claim oneness with the Creator and all of its goodness. An atheist could affirm that it is a beautiful universe, full of opportunity and infinite good and claim connection to all of this. The next thing to bring your mind into a place of oneness (denying separation from any of the Universe) is to affirm oneness with all of humanity and nature. I would affirm that I am a unique emanation of God and that I am made in its likeness of all "God Stuff." The third step is to blast yourself with affirmations. I like to use lots of them. I like to claim all of the great spiritual qualities and health and clarity for my mind, body, and spirit. The fourth step is gratitude. I have already paid homage to giving thanks and this fits into the treatment well. The fifth is to release it. This is to know that we don't need to force this outcome, and we can have the faith that we are in it, of it, and expressing this divinity now, without question. I will promise to post on YouTube with greater instruction for the process of Spiritual Mind Treatment. This is how I pray.

Naturally, getting busy on all this great stuff is essential and crucial. You may have heard...*God helps those who help themselves.* Of course, when your faith is relentless and your entire being is full of joy, living at a high vibration (with or without enough money), grace kicks in and opportunity knocks. I see it all the time and it works for anyone who is *all in.* If you doubt this, you can still do it the 'hard way.' Don't worry. It works when you are ready.

As your entire life elevates—-you find love, you make money, you are expressing fitness and health—-you find the need to make great decisions even more important. Expressing so many great qualities inspires one to want to be wiser and spread this joy in so many ways. I hope you share with me how this happens in your life.

Knowing what to ask for is always challenging, but it can be fun. I can offer an effective way to start.

First, visualize yourself exactly where you want to be. Picture it all as you wish it to be. You will need to be specific and make note of the details of what you have achieved and where you are. What do you do and where do you live? Who do you live with? Now, before you get overwhelmed, figure out what it is that you need to accomplish first. Document this in a separate file. You can expand upon the details of each file. You can create all of this, but remember the riddle, *how do you eat an elephant?* The answer is *one bite at a time.* If you have not heard of this, apply it here anyway, because it is appropriate.

So, pick your first needed piece of the puzzle, *or bite of the elephant.* Visualize how you created this piece to be enjoyed. Think backwards from the vision of completion. Imagine how you accomplished this. The truth is, you may not know how to do this, but rather than allow that to stop you, imagine how you did it. Write down the steps. Read about other people and how they accomplished it. Learn how they technically accomplished this thing you want to do, and if no one has done it, read accounts of similar accomplishments.

Call it a 'project.'

You may not have the time you want to work on your endeavor, but try to find at least an hour a day to work on it. If you need to chop down a tree and don't have the energy to do it all at once, you can take several chops, come back tomorrow and chop some more...*and you know where I am going*, because if you don't quit, the task will be accomplished eventually. You can call it one chop at a time, *or one bite at a time*, or whatever resonates with you. The key is, DON'T QUIT. You will finish.

If you knew exactly how to do the thing you are questioning, you would have perhaps done it already; this may be what you are thinking. Well, the truth is, things never really go as planned. Some of the things that you think are easy will be challenging, and some of the things that you think are impossible may go very well and quickly. You won't know the way until you get started. When one door closes, another opens, and you will invent a way if you stay focused and don't quit.

We are beginning to articulate a mindset. Let me make this part clear; you won't do everything in the process correctly. There will be mistakes, but if you can hold a mindset, you will be successful, despite your mistakes and lack of experience. I will give you a list, so it will be perfectly clear.

1. Don't allow fear, doubt or worry to get near your project. If you allow a little bit of doubt into your project, it will begin to wither, until it dissipates.

2. Know that you are worthy to accomplish your goal or project. If you feel unworthy, please get some therapy. You *are* worthy and will do great things as you accomplish the goal. Make those things part of your vision. Remove self-imposed barriers and improve your self-esteem. Do the free therapies on my website **CieScott.com** or talk it out with a therapist that won't

allow any victim consciousness. Many do, so avoid these therapists.

3. Make your project sacred. Don't allow friends or relatives to add their own flavor to your recipe. Don't speak about it with people that will not want you to succeed or have other plans for you. Studies have been completed that explain that declaring what you are about to create will bring worse results than if you keep it to yourself. You might think that if you declare it, you will be forced to perform, but statistics do not show this. You can do it either way, but I would not put my project out there for people to kick and abuse. Share it only with a few people who want a higher level of success for you. There will be rejection anyway. You will experience rejection on your path, but this will only send you in the correct direction, because you will find that when people don't want to deal with you, you are better off without them. Another option or path will appear, and you can continue. Know that it is for the best.

4. Be a person of action. Implement your ideas; talk is cheap. There are more ways than ever to find financial backers, so there are no excuses.

5. Your desire will aid in drawing you forward, even when you must fail forward. Chances are very small that you can sail forward into success without some failures, but remember, failure is another word for experience, and experience is very valuable. Remember not to think of failing as loss.

6. Don't quit. You don't really fail until you quit, so cross the finish line.

Visualize yourself victorious; you have crossed the finish line. Now tell yourself, *how did you get there?* Plot out the most likely way to get from where you are-Point A to Point B, but start at B and tell the story of your imagined success backwards. Start by working backwards from your vision. You will see how amazingly intuitive you are. Turn within, as in Step #6. Trust your instincts. Draw out your finished puzzle and examine those pieces, then create them and put them into your "project puzzle." This is your starting point. Continue, piece by piece.

True, it is somewhat doubtful that you will be able to predict how you created each piece and how the pieces fit into the puzzle to build your dream. If you are 100% committed, not 99.5% but fully committed, it is possible to do it with or without knowing a lot about the pieces of the puzzle. When you let even a small amount, *less than 1%* of fear, doubt or worry into your recipe, it will stop you.

What do you do when you are all in, invested, time was spent, resources are engaged and doubt or difficulties enter your plan? I will tell you the same thing I would tell you if you were losing weight on a diet and ate a big piece of chocolate cake. Forgive yourself. Start again tomorrow with your best attitude.

Here is the bottom line on mysticism; a mystic is not psychic. Mystics don't read cards or read your palm.

I am a mystic, but I don't predict the future, per se. In my (therapy) practice, a patient can tell me a story, and before they get to the end, I will ask if they want to finish it or if they want me to tell the ending. This surprises them, but when I have my mind around the situation and the beliefs of the patient, it's easy to know how the story ends. This is a mystical talent, perhaps, but I describe it this way—when I know what a person does, based on their beliefs, emotions and actions, I know if things work well or work poorly, and very often I can guess how the story ends with confidence.

If you decide to look up the definition of mysticism, you will get several answers. These answers may include psychic abilities, but I don't trust in psychic abilities, per se. The elements of definitions that I find true include these (from Cambridge Dictionary and Merriam-Webster) and some of my own:

- belief that direct knowledge of God, spiritual truth, or ultimate reality can be attained through subjective experience

- mysticism may include intuition or insight and serious contemplation, through quiet consideration

- the belief that it is possible to directly obtain truth or achieve communication with God or other forces controlling the Universe by prayer and contemplation

- a theory postulating the possibility of direct and intuitive acquisition of ineffable knowledge

- the belief that there is hidden meaning in life or that each human being is united with God

After you invest yourself deeply into spiritual practice, you will be a mystic too. Practice is the way. Do it and live it. Spiritual practice includes meditation, prayer, affirmations, visualization, and daily gratitude. You may not wish to do all of these, but, *whatever you do*, don't neglect gratitude. A fool can prosper with gratitude.

CONTINUE FORWARD WITH YOUR PERFECT DECISIONS

Staying focused is a skill, but we can all master this. I promise. We all have a little ADD as well as distractions; none of us can use these as excuses. I have friends that cannot read well due to neurological disorders, yet they have created businesses valued at over $20 million without start-up capital. *What would you do if you had no limitations?* When you are aligned with your purpose and the enrichment that is virtually free and all around you, you *can* succeed. *Don't forget,* your limitations are imagined.

Decide to persevere.

Your decisions need a commitment to back them. This is what gives your decision real power. Your follow-through will dictate your success and failure. You give your decision power and value. Decisions without execution are worthless. Commitment is a huge element of power, and I might also say power is a huge element of commitment. If you have decided not to smoke, being a non-smoker will take commitment. The power of your decision will bring you better health, better karma, and a financial savings if you need not purchase cigarettes. Quitting such habits always takes commitment. Those who abandon their promises have lower self-esteem and will not achieve their goals. "Don't be a quitter," my father always said to me. More so, you can decide not to be a failure ever again. Using these important instructions leads to success or at least another necessary experience moving you closer to success. By standing by your decisions and steadfastly carrying them out, you will find yourself a winner rather than a quitter. The dividend for following through and finishing is another boost in self-esteem.

Persistence has many benefits. Whether it is relationships, physical work-outs, proper eating, selling, or creating, persistence is one of the keys to success.

In sales, as well as in finding a mate, we must endure or follow through. If the first attempt at a sale is declined, try again. My father was a teacher and a very tough college basketball coach. I'm reminding you again of his words: "Quitters never win and winners never quit." Your style with anything will improve with practice. You cannot argue that ten no's and one yes is better than two no's.

When you receive the 'no' reply, just move on to the next. Your pitch will improve as you go. You're one step closer to a 'yes.' Life is a series of numbers games. Be persistent and it will be possible to achieve anything.

F.Y.I.: Perseverance is not annoyance. It is continuance with commitment. With commitment, anything is possible.

Let's lessen the challenge of perseverance. Consider the desired outcome-- will your task help you or others? If so, put your fears aside. First, identify your fears. Secondly, realize these fears are "crazy thinking" and very simply negative energy. Tell those negative or lazy thoughts to get lost. Winning support is an easier task when we accept the probability of some rejection. Rejection is not a problem. It is a challenge that can bring forth a valuable lesson. The 'song and dance' or pitch we wish to deliver is a numbers game. Every 'no' answer advances us toward the next 'yes.' If we choose not to hear the "crazy thinking," we can push through the numbers toward the victories. Breakdowns lead to breakthroughs. Breakthroughs are only available to those who don't give up.

There is a cost for not persevering.

No growth=No achievement=No accomplishment

We also feel weaker when the next challenge arises. It's like lifting weights to body sculpt or build. There are no exceptions to this rule. Everyone has to work his way up to the heavy weights. **Strength and endurance come with time and effort.** They also return with time and effort. **Attaining goals will definitely be worth every challenge.**

The most difficult challenge is waiting. There is no telling how long it will take to reach the goal. Use the other distinctions in this section of the book to minimize the time necessary. You may rewrite the goal, but never give up. Unrealized expectations can lead to quitting. Keep the possibility open rather than fixing on an expectation. **Being open to possibility always leaves the dream intact.**

Trust the flow of the Universe and the bigger picture will be revealed at the time it will serve most successfully.

Decide to subscribe to my final *CIEcret:*

It is common to feel we cannot reach far enough to attain something. It could be a relationship, a fit body, money, a job, or a new business.

We as individuals are truly part of "The Big Picture." The "domino effect" is real; lack and limitations are only illusions.

Dream your dream and get started on it. There are no excuses.

Take a minute to inhale all the Universe has to offer... and don't forget to exhale your smallness, since it's only imagined.

Life is what you make it.

Choose well, my friend.

About the author....

Dr. Cie Scott is a "Media Psychologist", author, and International Keynote Speaker. Dr. Cie has over twenty-five years of experience as an actress, TV host and narrator, including voice-overs for more than 100 productions. Dr. Cie is a seasoned television producer who has successfully transitioned from working in 'front of the camera' to working, 'behind the camera'. A published author of both text and audio books, she is also the writer of TV commercials, infomercials, episodic and "how to" daytime TV programs, music videos, and thought-provoking, "Dr. Cie Tips" for the body, mind, and spirit.

Once specializing in Direct Response advertising, she uses her degree in Psychology to influence and inspire television viewers. With experience as a powerful teacher, Cie's careers in modeling, acting, and hosting, afforded her a unique education which included improvisation and comedy. She played prankster parts on Totally Hidden Video, Saturday Night Live, and also performed stand-up comedy at The Improv in L.A. Cie understands the value of a comedic edge and uses humor divinely in hundreds of celebrity interviews for FOX, ABC, CBS, and UPN television.

Feeling creatively incomplete reading lines for recurring roles on General Hospital, Baywatch, and many other episodics, her self-expression took over and she created Infinite Power, a daytime TV show which she grew from three markets to 186 on major networks. Executive Producing her show afforded her the opportunity to learn most TV production jobs and successfully syndicate her own show. Focused on her tasks, she became an excellent writer; advertising clients were also pleased with her ability to research and execute meaningful scripts. As a former owner of a production company, she also produced commercials for large, world-wide companies such as LifeFitness, Toto, and Stevia. She has created and produced martial arts videos, exercise videos, as well as TV pilots, such as The Most Beautiful Women in the World, with Tippi Hedron and Gena Lee Nolan.

Dr. Cie Scott now cherry picks TV and film projects, writes inspiring self-help books and magazine columns, and is a voting member of the Academy of Television Arts and Sciences. She is also a member of both SAG and AFTRA. She currently spends much of her time lecturing throughout the world and appearing as a television host or guest, offering "info-tainment" and lively, enlightening self -help. As an actress, TV host and producer, "Dr. Cie" earned 8 Tellys, 2 Vision Awards, and 2 Emmy nominations for production and hosting.

Dr. Cie lives with her husband of over 15 years and her three Papillons, also serving as Therapy Dogs in the community.

More to Cie...
www.CieScott.com
www.FastTherapy.com
www.JetSetPHD.com
www.CelebritiesWithHeart.com
www.InfinitePowerTV.com
www.TheWellnessDocs.com

Also by Cie Allman Scott, Ph. D.

<u>THE PEOPLE MAGNET</u> (CD Audio book) ISBN 10: 0-9774811-1-5   ISBN 13: 978097748118) 2009
Listen Today! Attract Immediately! Flip the switch to success! Realize 21 keys to relate better to others, and enjoy a better connection with all people when you 'remove the static.'
If you're coming up short in life---no committed partner, no great clients, or maybe you just want to attract people to date, or to nail a good job---you may need a People Magnet! You can release and extend your magnetic power! This audio book will improve your relationships, finances, and health! Attract in every trajectory, energizing the Law of Attraction; you will easily comprehend 21 principled strategies or simple changes you can implement immediately to remove barriers and connect to others! You will also instantly enjoy a happier and more confident demeanor. You can stop repelling people, money, and vitally important health! Unblock your true Infinite Power today with THE PEOPLE MAGNET!

<u>REINVENT YOURSELF</u> (CD Audio book/ Audio Download) ISBN: 9780966225730
Earn big money without competition by doing what you love!
Finding your purpose aligns you with doing what you love and getting paid! Enjoy easy and fun exercises to find your purpose and happiness in under 30 minutes! Use this passion to create your dream job! As you work for yourself, you forge a career that resonates with you and your genuine inner enthusiasm! Affirmations and guided meditation tracks reduce fear and empower every user; these tracks can be used every day! This product facilitates instant clarity and confidence, self respect, self-awareness, and breakthroughs! The process is easy to do anywhere and can be effective every time in your life you need to progress with paradigm shifts, and reinvent yourself again.

THE GODDESS CODE Your Secret Weapon for Dating Success! ISBN 13: 978-0-94811-4-9 (Audio download)

The Goddess Code is the single girls' therapy and guidance for successful dating, straight from the host of The Goddess Code, on iTunes, Stitcher.com, YouTube and Facebook Live! You can establish trust and commitment with a KEEPER and FORGET the losers forever! IT is 100% effective for repairing your self esteem and putting you on the correct path to find the one you desire. The Goddess Code works for young and old. It works for all genders. Dr. Cie Scott interviewed over 20,000 singles coast to coast, who were seeking "THE ONE". These men and women provided the groundwork for the keys to find commitment in a world of serial monogamy, pain, and disrespect! Find timeless, perfect answers immediately and useful keys to create the life you want to live and the path to your loving partner! These keys to commitment are EXPLICIT and CRYSTAL CLEAR, so implementing them immediately creates instant dating success and order in your life. Want to know if someone is truthful with you? Never put your self respect on the line and never lose control again! Get started today! Gain the confidence and clarity you need to find a winner in a sea of undesirable partners. Reduce your stress level and stop struggling with THE GODDESS CODE; it's your secret weapon! Stop your harmful patterns today! This special release goes beyond the podcast and free information, and if you are finished making mistakes, you can't afford to skip over it!

MEDITATION FOR BEGINNERS and INTERMEDIATE: Natural Stress Release, Anti-Aging and Self Realization (CD Audio book/Audio Download) ISBN: 978-0-977481132

Guided Meditations and easy instruction allow you to meditate and overcome previous obstacles in this simple, pleasurable process. Deep relaxation techniques allow you to rejuvenate for better overall health, and clarity results from this daily meditation habit!

Instant gratification:
- Tranquility and Unshakable Confidence
- Creative Solutions & Clarity of Mind
- Increased Energy and Better Health
- Discover Daily Peace
- Improve Your Relationships & Finances

POWERFUL DAILY AFFIRMATIONS FOR SUCCESS
(CD/Audio Download)
Listen daily for transformation, inspiration and unshakable confidence! Relax, listen and repeat after Dr. Cie! You can reprogram the negativity you have collected over time and find a confident outlook on life that lasts and alters your future for the better.

You can find most audio downloads at **TheAudioBookMarket.com** and check my "Tool Box" (online store) at **CieScott.com** or **Amazon.com**

More resources...

YouTube channels:

Cie Allman-Scott for Body, Mind & Spirit tips and many Infinite Power TV episodes, previously broadcast on TV
Cie Scott for Celebrity Interviews, Exclusive Emmy parties and other Jet Set PHD travel tips

Write to me with your inspiring story at this address:

"Dr. Cie"
11811 N. Tatum Blvd.
Suite 3031
Phoenix, AZ 85028

I love this; I live this…

"*A hundred times every day I remind myself that my inner and outer life are based on the labors of other men, living and dead, and that I must exert myself in order to give in the same measure as I have received and am still receiving.*"

~ Albert Einstein